The Companion Species Manifesto

The Companion Species Manifesto:
Dogs, People, and Significant Otherness

Donna Haraway

PRICKLY PARADIGM PRESS
CHICAGO

Short excerpts from this pamphlet appear courtesy of
Indiana University Press.

Prickly Paradigm Press, LLC
5629 South University Avenue
Chicago, Il 60637

www.prickly-paradigm.com

ISBN: 0-9717575-8-5
LCCN: 2002115995

Seventh printing March 2020

Printed in the United States of America on acid-free
paper.

For Rusten and all of our companions

Emergent Naturecultures

From "Notes of a Sports Writer's Daughter":

> *Ms Cayenne Pepper continues to colonize all my cells—a sure case of what the biologist Lynn Margulis calls symbiogenesis. I bet if you checked our DNA, you'd find some potent transfections between us. Her saliva must have the viral vectors. Surely, her darter-tongue kisses have been irresistible. Even though we share placement in the phylum of vertebrates, we inhabit not just different genera and divergent families, but altogether different orders.*
>
> *How would we sort things out? Canid, hominid; pet, professor; bitch, woman; animal, human; athlete, handler. One of us has a microchip injected under her neck skin for identification; the other has a photo ID*

California driver's license. One of us has a written record of her ancestors for twenty generations; one of us does not know her great grandparents' names. One of us, product of a vast genetic mixture, is called "pure-bred." One of us, equally product of a vast mixture, is called "white." Each of these names designates a racial discourse, and we both inherit their consequences in our flesh.

One of us is at the cusp of flaming, youthful, phys-ical achievement; the other is lusty but over the hill. And we play a team sport called agility on the same expropriated Native land where Cayenne's ancestors herded merino sheep. These sheep were imported from the already colonial pastoral economy of Australia to feed the California Gold Rush 49ers. In layers of history, layers of biology, layers of naturecultures, complexity is the name of our game. We are both the freedom-hungry offspring of conquest, products of white settler colonies, leaping over hurdles and crawling through tunnels on the playing field.

I'm sure our genomes are more alike than they should be. There must be some molecular record of our touch in the codes of living that will leave traces in the world, no matter that we are each reproductively silenced females, one by age, one by surgery. Her red merle Australian Shepherd's quick and lithe tongue has swabbed the tissues of my tonsils, with all their eager immune system receptors. Who knows where my chem-ical receptors carried her messages, or what she took from my cellular system for distinguishing self from other and binding outside to inside?

We have had forbidden conversation; we have had oral intercourse; we are bound in telling story upon story with nothing but the facts. We are training each other in acts of communication we barely understand. We are, constitutively, companion species. We make each

other up, in the flesh. Significantly other to each other,
in specific difference, we signify in the flesh a nasty
developmental infection called love. This love is an
historical aberration and a naturalcultural legacy.

This manifesto explores two questions flowing
from this aberration and legacy: 1) how might an
ethics and politics committed to the flourishing of
significant otherness be learned from taking dog-
human relationships seriously; and 2) how might
stories about dog-human worlds finally convince
brain-damaged US Americans, and maybe other less
historically challenged people, that history matters in
naturecultures?

The Companion Species Manifesto is a personal
document, a scholarly foray into too many half known
territories, a political act of hope in a world on the
edge of global war, and a work permanently in
progress, in principle. I offer dog-eaten props and
half-trained arguments to reshape some stories I care
about a great deal, as a scholar and as a person in my
time and place. The story here is mainly about dogs.
Passionately engaged in these accounts, I hope to
bring my readers into the kennel for life. But I hope
also that even the dog phobic—or just those with their
minds on higher things—will find arguments and
stories that matter to the worlds we might yet live in.
The practices and actors in dog worlds, human and
non-human alike, ought to be central concerns of
technoscience studies. Even closer to my heart, I want
my readers to know why I consider dog writing to be a
branch of feminist theory, or the other way around.

4

This is not my first manifesto; in 1985, I
published "The Cyborg Manifesto" to try to make
feminist sense of the implosions of contemporary life
in technoscience. Cyborgs are "cybernetic organisms,"
named in 1960 in the context of the space race, the
cold war, and imperialist fantasies of technohumanism
built into policy and research projects. I tried to
inhabit cyborgs critically; i.e., neither in celebration
nor condemnation, but in a spirit of ironic appropria-
tion for ends never envisioned by the space warriors.
Telling a story of co-habitation, co-evolution, and
embodied cross-species sociality, the present manifesto
asks which of two cobbled together figures—cyborgs
and companion species—might more fruitfully inform
livable politics and ontologies in current life worlds.
These figures are hardly polar opposites. Cyborgs and
companion species each bring together the human and
non-human, the organic and technological, carbon
and silicon, freedom and structure, history and myth,
the rich and the poor, the state and the subject, diversity and depletion, modernity and postmodernity, and
nature and culture in unexpected ways. Besides,
neither a cyborg nor a companion animal pleases the
pure of heart who long for better protected species
boundaries and sterilization of category deviants.
Nonetheless, the differences between even the most
politically correct cyborg and an ordinary dog matter.

I appropriated cyborgs to do feminist work in
Reagan's Star Wars times of the mid-1980s. By the
end of the millennium, cyborgs could no longer do
the work of a proper herding dog to gather up the
threads needed for critical inquiry. So I go happily to

the dogs to explore the birth of the kennel to help craft tools for science studies and feminist theory in the present time, when secondary Bushes threaten to replace the old growth of more livable naturecultures in the carbon budget politics of all water-based life on earth. Having worn the scarlet letters, "Cyborgs for earthly survival!" long enough, I now brand myself with a slogan only Schutzhund women from dog sports could have come up with, when even a first nip can result in a death sentence: "Run fast; bite hard!"

This is a story of biopower and biosociality, as well as of technoscience. Like any good Darwinian, I tell a story of evolution. In the mode of (nucleic) acidic millennialism, I tell a tale of molecular differences, but one less rooted in Mitochondrial Eve in a neocolonial *Out of Africa* and more rooted in those first mitochondrial canine bitches who got in the way of man making himself yet again in the Greatest Story Ever Told. Instead, those bitches insisted on the history of companion species, a very mundane and ongoing sort of tale, one full of misunderstandings, achievements, crimes, and renewable hopes. Mine is a story told by a student of the sciences and a feminist of a certain generation who has gone to the dogs, literally. Dogs, in their historical complexity, matter here. Dogs are not an alibi for other themes; dogs are fleshly material-semiotic presences in the body of technoscience. Dogs are not surrogates for theory; they are not here just to think with. They are here to live with. Partners in the crime of human evolution, they are in the garden from the get-go, wily as Coyote.

Prehensions

Many versions of process philosophies help me walk with my dogs in this manifesto. For example, Alfred North Whitehead described "the concrete" as "a concrescence of prehensions." For him, "the concrete" meant an "actual occasion." Reality is an active verb, and the nouns all seem to be gerunds with more appendages than an octopus. Through their reaching into each other, through their "prehensions" or graspings, beings constitute each other and themselves. Beings do not preexist their relatings. "Prehensions" have consequences. The world is a knot in motion. Biological and cultural determinism are both instances of misplaced concreteness—i.e., the mistake of, first, taking provisional and local category abstractions like "nature" and "culture" for the world and, second, mistaking potent consequences to be preexisting foundations. There are no pre-constituted subjects and objects, and no single sources, unitary actors, or final ends. In Judith Butler's terms, there are only "contingent foundations;" bodies that matter are the result. A bestiary of agencies, kinds of relatings, and scores of time trump the imaginings of even the most baroque cosmologists. For me, that is what *companion species* signifies.

My love of Whitehead is rooted in biology, but even more in the practice of feminist theory as I have experienced it. This feminist theory, in its refusal of typological thinking, binary dualisms, and both relativisms and universalisms of many flavors, contributes a rich array of approaches to emergence, process, historicity, difference, specificity, co-habitation, co-constitution, and contingency. Dozens of feminist writers have refused both relativism and universalism. Subjects, objects, kinds, races, species, genres, and genders are the products of their relating. None of this work is about finding sweet and nice— "feminine"—worlds and knowledges free of the ravages and productivities of power. Rather, feminist inquiry is about understanding how things work, who is in the action, what might be possible, and how worldly actors might somehow be accountable to and love each other less violently.

For example, studying Yoruba- and English-speaking mathematics elementary school classrooms in post-independence Nigeria and participating in Australian Aboriginal projects in math teaching and environmental policy, Helen Verran identifies "emergent ontologies." Verran asks "simple" questions: How can people rooted in different knowledge practices "get on together," especially when an all-too-easy cultural relativism is not an option, either politically, epistemologically, or morally? How can general knowledge be nurtured in postcolonial worlds committed to taking difference seriously? Answers to these questions can only be put together in emergent practices; i.e., in vulnerable, on-the-ground work that cobbles together non-harmonious agencies and ways of living that are accountable both to their disparate inherited histories and to their barely possible but absolutely necessary joint futures. For me, that is what *significant otherness* signifies.

Studying assisted reproduction practices in San Diego and then conservation science and politics in Kenya, Charis (Cussins) Thompson suggested the term "ontological choreographies." The scripting of the dance of being is more than a metaphor; bodies, human and non-human, are taken apart and put together in processes that make self-certainty and either humanist or organicist ideology bad guides to ethics and politics, much less to personal experience.

Finally, Marilyn Strathern, drawing on decades of study of Papua New Guinean histories and politics, as well as on her investigation of English kin-reckoning habits, taught us why conceiving of "nature" and "culture" as either polar opposites or universal categories is foolish. An ethnographer of relational categories, she showed how to think in other topologies. Instead of opposites, we get the whole sketchpad of the modern geometrician's fevered brain with which to draw relationality. Strathern thinks in terms of "partial connections;" i.e., patterns within which the players are neither wholes nor parts. I call these the relations of significant otherness. I think of Strathern as an ethnographer of naturecultures; she will not mind if I invite her into the kennel for a cross-species conversation.

For feminist theorists, who and what are in the world is precisely what is at stake. This is very promising philosophical bait for training us all to understand companion species in both storied deep time, which is chemically etched in the DNA of every cell, and in recent doings, which leave more odoriferous traces. In old-fashioned terms, *The Companion*

Species Manifesto is a kinship claim, one made possible by the concrescence of prehensions of many actual occasions. Companion species rest on contingent foundations.

And like the productions of a decadent gardener who can't keep good distinctions between natures and cultures straight, the shape of my kin networks looks more like a trellis or an esplanade than a tree. You can't tell up from down, and everything seems to go sidewise. Such snake-like, sidewinding traffic is one of my themes. My garden is full of snakes, full of trellises, full of indirection. Instructed by evolutionary population biologists and bioanthropologists, I know that multidirectional gene flow—multidirectional flows of bodies and values—is and has always been the name of the game of life on earth. It is certainly the way into the kennel. Whatever else humans and dogs can illustrate, it is that these large-bodied, globally distributed, ecologically opportunistic, gregariously social, mammalian co-travelers have written into their genomes a record of couplings and infectious exchanges to set the teeth of even the most committed free trader on edge. Even in the Galapagos Islands of the modern purebred dog fancy—where the effort to isolate and fragment breeding populations and deplete their heritage of diversity can look like model experiments for mimicking the natural disasters of population bottlenecks and epidemic disease—the restless exuberance of gene flow cannot be stilled. Impressed by this traffic, I risk alienating my old doppelgänger, the cyborg, in order to try to convince readers that dogs might be better guides through the thickets of technobiopolitics in the Third Millennium of the Current Era.

Companions

In "The Cyborg Manifesto," I tried to write a surrogacy agreement, a trope, a figure for living within and honoring the skills and practices of contemporary technoculture without losing touch with the permanent war apparatus of a non-optional, post-nuclear world and its transcendent, very material lies. Cyborgs can be figures for living within contradictions, attentive to the naturecultures of mundane practices, opposed to the dire myths of self-birthing, embracing mortality as the condition for life, and alert to the emergent historical hybridities actually populating the world at all its contingent scales.

However, cyborg refigurations hardly exhaust the tropic work required for ontological choreography in technoscience. I have come to see cyborgs as junior siblings in the much bigger, queer family of companion species, in which reproductive biotechno-politics are generally a surprise, sometimes even a nice surprise. I know that a US middle-aged white woman with a dog playing the sport of agility is no match for the automated warriors, terrorists, and their transgenic kin in the annals of philosophical inquiry or the ethnography of naturecultures. Besides, 1) self-figuration is not my task; 2) transgenics are not the enemy; and 3) contrary to lots of dangerous and unethical projection in the Western world that makes domestic canines into furry children, dogs are not about oneself. Indeed, that is the beauty of dogs. They are not a projection, nor the realization of an intention, nor the telos of anything. They are dogs; i.e., a species in obligatory, constitutive, historical, protean relationship with human beings. The relationship is not especially nice; it is full of waste, cruelty, indifference, ignorance, and loss, as well as of joy, invention, labor, intelligence, and play. I want to learn how to narrate this co-history and how to inherit the consequences of co-evolution in natureculture.

There cannot be just one companion species; there have to be at least two to make one. It is in the syntax; it is in the flesh. Dogs are about the inescapable, contradictory story of relationships—co-constitutive relationships in which none of the partners pre-exist the relating, and the relating is never done once and for all. Historical specificity and contingent mutability rule all the way down, into nature and culture, into naturecultures. There is no foundation; there are only elephants supporting elephants all the way down.

Companion animals comprise only one kind of companion species, and neither category is very old in American English. In United States English, the term "companion animal" emerges in medical and psycho-sociological work in veterinary schools and related sites from the middle 1970s. This research told us that, except for those few non-dog loving New Yorkers who obsess about unscooped dog shit in the streets, having a dog lowers one's blood pressure and ups one's chances of surviving childhood, surgery, and divorce.

Certainly, references in European languages to animals serving as companions, rather than as working or sporting dogs, predate this US biomedical, technoscientific literature by centuries. Further, in China, Mexico, and elsewhere in the ancient and contemporary world, the documentary, archaeological, and oral evidence for dogs as pets, in addition to a myriad of other jobs, is strong. In the early Americas dogs assisted in hauling, hunting, and herding for various peoples. For others, dogs were food or a source of fleece. Dog people like to forget that dogs were also lethal guided weapons and instruments of terror in the European conquest of the Americas, as well as in Alexander the Great's paradigm-setting imperial travels. With combat history in Viet Nam as an officer in the US marines, Akita breeder and dog writer John Cargill reminds us that before cyborg warfare, trained dogs were among the best intelligent weapons systems. And tracking hounds terrorized slaves and prisoners, as well as rescued lost children and earthquake victims.

Listing these functions does not begin to get at the heterogeneous history of dogs in symbol and story all over the world, nor does the list of jobs tell us how dogs were treated or how they regarded their human associates. In *A History of Dogs in the Early Americas* (Yale, 1997), Marion Schwartz writes that some American Indian hunting dogs went through similar rituals of preparation as did their humans, including among the Achuar of South America the ingestion of an hallucinogen. In *In the Company of Animals* (Cambridge, 1986), James Serpell relates that for the nineteenth-century Comanche of the Great Plains, horses were of great practical value. But horses were treated in a utilitarian way, while dogs, kept as pets, merited fond stories and warriors mourned their deaths. Some dogs were and are vermin; some were and are buried like people. Contemporary Navajo herding dogs relate to their landscape, their sheep, their people, coyotes, and dog or human strangers in historically specific ways. In cities, villages, and rural areas all over the world, many dogs live parallel lives among people, more or less tolerated, sometimes used and sometimes abused. No one term can do justice to this history.

However, the term "companion animal" enters US technoculture through the post-Civil War land-grant academic institutions housing the vet schools. That is, "companion animal" has the pedigree of the mating between technoscientific expertise and late industrial pet-keeping practices, with their democratic masses in love with their domestic partners, or at least with the non-human ones. Companion animals can be horses, dogs, cats, or a range of other beings willing to make the leap to the biosociality of service dogs, family members, or team members in cross-species sports. Generally speaking, one does not eat one's companion animals (nor get eaten by them); and one has a hard time shaking colonialist, ethnocentric, ahistorical attitudes toward those who do (eat or get eaten).

Species

"Companion species" is a bigger and more heterogeneous category than companion animal, and not just because one must include such organic beings as rice, bees, tulips, and intestinal flora, all of whom make life for humans what it is—and vice versa. I want to write the keyword entry for "companion species" to insist on four tones simultaneously resonating in the linguistic, historical voice box that enables uttering this term. First, as a dutiful daughter of Darwin, I insist on the tones of the history of evolutionary biology, with its categories of populations, rates of gene flow, variation, selection, and biological species. The debates in the last 150 years about whether the category "species" denotes a real biological entity or merely figures a convenient taxonomic box sound the over- and undertones. Species is about biological kind, and scientific expertise is necessary to that kind of reality. Post-cyborg, what counts as biological kind troubles previous categories of organism. The machinic and the textual are internal to the organic and vice versa in irreversible ways.

Second, schooled by Thomas Aquinas and other Aristotelians, I remain alert to species as generic philosophical kind and category. Species is about defining difference, rooted in polyvocal fugues of doctrines of cause.

Third, my soul indelibly marked by a Catholic formation, I hear in species the doctrine of the Real Presence under both species, bread and wine, the transubstantiated signs of the flesh. Species is about the corporeal join of the material and the semiotic in ways unacceptable to the secular Protestant sensibilities of the American academy and to most versions of the human science of semiotics.

Fourth, converted by Marx and Freud and a sucker for dubious etymologies, I hear in species filthy lucre, specie, gold, shit, filth, wealth. In *Love's Body*, Norman O. Brown taught me about the join of Marx and Freud in shit and gold, in primitive scat and civilized metal, in specie. I met this join again in modern US dog culture, with its exuberant commodity culture; its vibrant practices of love and desire; its structures that tie together the state, civil society, and the liberal individual; its mongrel technologies of purebred subject- and object-making. As I glove my hand in the plastic film—courtesy of the research empires of industrial chemistry—that protects my morning *New York Times* to pick up the microcosmic ecosystems, called scat, produced anew each day by my dogs, I find pooper scoopers quite a joke, one that lands me back in the histories of the incarnation, political economy, technoscience, and biology.

In sum, "companion species" is about a four-part composition, in which co-constitution, finitude, impurity, historicity, and complexity are what is.

The Companion Species Manifesto is, thus, about the implosion of nature and culture in the relentlessly historically specific, joint lives of dogs and people, who are bonded in significant otherness. Many are interpellated into that story, and the tale is instructive also for those who try to keep a hygienic distance. I want to convince my readers that inhabitants of technoculture become who we are in the symbiogenetic tissues of naturecultures, in story and in fact.

I take "interpellation" from the French post-structuralist and Marxist philosopher Louis Althusser's theory for how subjects are constituted from concrete individuals by being "hailed" through ideology into their subject positions in the modern state. Today, through our ideologically loaded narratives of their lives, animals "hail" us to account for the regimes in which they and we must live. We "hail" them into our constructs of nature and culture, with major consequences of life and death, health and illness, longevity and extinction. We also live with each other in the flesh in ways not exhausted by our ideologies. Stories are much bigger than ideologies. In that is our hope.

In this long philosophical introduction, I am violating a major rule of "Notes of a Sports Writer's Daughter," my doggish scribblings in honor of my sports writer father, which pepper this manifesto. The "Notes" require there to be no deviation from the animal stories themselves. Lessons have to be inextricably part of the story; it's a rule of truth as a genre for those of us—practicing and lapsed Catholics and their fellow travelers—who believe that the sign and the flesh are one.

Reporting the facts, telling a true story, I write "Notes of a Sports Writer's Daughter." A sports writer's job is, or at least was, to report the game story. I know this because as a child I sat in the press box in the AAA baseball club's Denver Bears' Stadium late at night watching my father write and file his game stories. A sports writer, perhaps more than other news people, has a curious job—to tell what happened by spinning a story that is just the facts. The more vivid the prose, the better; indeed, if crafted faithfully, the more potent the tropes, the truer the story. My father did not want to have a sports column, a more prestigious activity in the newspaper business. He wanted to write the game stories, to stay close to the action, to tell it like it is, not to look for the scandals and the angles for the meta-story, the column. My father's faith was in the game, where fact and story cohabit.

I grew up in the bosom of two major institutions that counter the modernist belief in the no-fault divorce, based on irrevocable differences, of story and fact. Both of these institutions—the Church and the Press—are famously corrupt, famously scorned (if constantly used) by Science, and nonetheless indispensable in cultivating a people's insatiable hunger for truth. Sign and flesh; story and fact. In my natal house, the generative partners could not separate. They were, in down-and-dirty dog talk, tied. No wonder culture and nature imploded for me as an adult. And nowhere did that implosion have more force than in living the relationship and speaking the verb that passes as a noun: companion species. Is this what John meant when he said, "The Word was made flesh"? In the bottom of the ninth inning, the Bears down by two runs, with three on, two out, and two strikes, with the time deadline for filing the story five minutes away?

I also grew up in the house of Science and learned at around the time my breast buds erupted about how many underground passages there are connecting the Estates and how many couplings keep sign and flesh, story and fact, together in the palaces of positive knowledge, falsifiable hypothesis, and synthesizing theory. Because my science was biology, I learned early that accounting for evolution, development, cellular function, genome complexity, the molding of form across time, behavioral ecology, systems communication, cognition—in short, accounting for anything worthy of the name of biology—was not so different from getting a game story filed or living with the conundrums of the incarnation. To do biology with any kind of fidelity, the practitioner *must* tell a story, *must* get the facts, and *must* have the heart to stay hungry for the truth and to abandon a favorite story, a favorite fact, shown to be somehow off the mark. The practitioner must also have the heart to stay with a story through thick and thin, to inherit its discordant resonances, to live its contradictions, when that story gets at a truth about life that matters. Isn't that kind of fidelity what has made the science of evolutionary biology flourish and feed my people's corporeal hunger for knowledge over the last hundred and fifty years?

Etymologically, facts refer to performance, action, deeds done—feats, in short. A fact is a past participle, a thing done, over, fixed, shown, performed, accomplished. Facts have made the deadline for getting into the next edition of the paper. Fiction, etymologically, is very close, but differs by part-of-speech and tense. Like facts, fiction refers to action, but fiction is about the act of fashioning, forming, inventing, as well as feigning or feinting.

Drawn from a present participle, fiction is in process and still at stake, not finished, still prone to falling afoul of facts, but also liable to showing something we do not yet know to be true, but will know. Living with animals, inhabiting their/our stories, trying to tell the truth about relationship, co-habiting an active history: that is the work of companion species, for whom "the relation" is the smallest possible unit of analysis.

So, I file dog stories for a living these days. All stories traffic in tropes, i.e., figures of speech necessary to say anything at all. Trope (Greek: *tropós*) means swerving or tripping. All language swerves and trips; there is never direct meaning; only the dogmatic think that trope-free communication is our province. My favorite trope for dog tales is "metaplasm." Metaplasm means a change in a word, for example by adding, omitting, inverting, or transposing its letters, syllables, or sounds. The term is from the Greek *metaplasmos*, meaning remodeling or remolding. Metaplasm is a generic term for almost any kind of alteration in a word, intentional or unintentional. I use metaplasm to mean the remodeling of dog and human flesh, remolding the codes of life, in the history of companion-species relating.

Compare and contrast "protoplasm," "cytoplasm," "neoplasm," and "germplasm." There is a biological taste to "metaplasm"—just what I like in words about words. Flesh and signifier, bodies and words, stories and worlds: these are joined in naturecultures. Metaplasm can signify a mistake, a stumbling, a troping that makes a fleshly difference.

For example, a substitution in a string of bases in a nucleic acid can be a metaplasm, changing the meaning of a gene and altering the course of a life. Or, a remolded practice among dog breeders, such as doing more outcrosses and fewer close line breedings, could result from changed meanings of a word like "population" or "diversity." Inverting meanings; transposing the body of communication; remolding, remodeling; swervings that tell the truth: I tell stories about stories, all the way down. Woof.

Implicitly, this manifesto is about more than the relation of dogs and people. Dogs and people figure a universe. Clearly, cyborgs—with their historical congealings of the machinic and the organic in the codes of information, where boundaries are less about skin than about statistically defined densities of signal and noise—fit within the taxon of companion species. That is to say, cyborgs raise all the questions of histories, politics, and ethics that dogs require. Care, flourishing, differences in power, scales of time—these matter for cyborgs. For example, what kind of temporal scale-making could shape labor systems, investment strategies, and consumption patterns in which the generation time of information machines became compatible with the generation times of human, animal, and plant communities and ecosystems? What is the right kind of pooper-scooper for a computer or a personal digital assistant? At the least, we know it is not an electronics dump in Mexico or India, where human scavengers get paid less than nothing for processing the ecologically toxic waste of the well informed.

Art and engineering are natural sibling practices for engaging companion species. Thus, human-
landscape couplings fit snugly within the category of
companion species, evoking all the questions about the
histories and relatings that weld the souls of dogs and

*Figure 1. In the mid-1990s, this image of a ewe reversing life's
inequities by penning nine Border Collies graced a Ciba-Geigy adver-
tisement for its sheep and cattle flukicide and vermicide. Subject to the
hard eye and stalk of the camera, the UK national sheepdog trial cham-
pion Thomas Longton stands on his Quernmore farm in Lancashire
ready to close the pen on his accomplished dogs. Later, without the refer-
ence to Combinex but with a Dutch windmill airbrushed onto the landscape, a mirror image of the scene circulated widely in dogland on the
Internet. Without credits or identifying information, the photo bore the
apt title, "Border Collie Hell." Even without the relocated Dutch windmill, the photo was always a cyborg composite. For starters, two of the
dogs are repeats of the same individuals, but from different angles; the
young dogs in the rear are tied by invisible leads to the pen fence; the ewe
was melded into the scene from another photo. In* The Companion
Species Manifesto, *"Border Collie Hell" signals the ironic reversals
embedded in naturecultures. Animals, people, landscapes, corporations,
and technologies are all in on the joke. The photo also pleases those who
1) enjoyed the film* Babe, *and 2) work with herding dogs other than
Border Collies. Thanks to Thomas Longton for the ad brochure and the
story. Thanks also to webs of science studies, editorial, corporate, and
Border Collie people who helped me track everything down.*

their humans. The Scots sculptor Andrew Goldsworthy understands this well. Scales and flows of time through the flesh of plants, earth, sea, ice, and stone consume Goldsworthy. For him, the history of the land is living; and that history is composed out of the polyform relatings of people, animals, soil, water, and rocks. He works at scales of sculpted ice crystals interlaced with twigs, layered rock cones the size of a man built in the surging intertidal zones of the shore, and stone walls across long stretches of countryside. He has an engineer's and an artist's knowledge of forces like gravity and friction. His sculptures endure sometimes for seconds, sometimes for decades; but mortality and change are never out of consciousness. Process and dissolution—and agencies both human and non-human, as well as animate and inanimate— are his partners and materials, not just his themes.

In the 1990s, Goldsworthy did a work called *Arch*. He and writer David Craig traced an ancient drover's sheep route from Scottish pastures to an English market town. Photographing as they went, they assembled and disassembled a self-supporting red sandstone arch across places marking the past and present history of animals, people, and land. The missing trees and cottars, the story of the enclosures and rising wool markets, the fraught ties between England and Scotland over centuries, the conditions of possibility of the Scottish working sheepdog and hired shepherd, the sheep eating and walking to shearing and slaughter—these are memorialized in the moving rock arch tying together geography, history, and natural history.

The collie implicit in Goldsworthy's *Arch* is less about "Lassie come home" than "cottar get out." That is one condition of possibility of the immensely popular late twentieth-century British TV show about the brilliant working sheepdogs, the Border Collies of Scotland. Shaped genetically by competitive sheep trialing since the late nineteenth century, this breed has made that sport justly famous on several continents. This is the same breed of dog that dominates the sport of agility in my life. It is also the breed that is thrown away in large numbers to be rescued by dedicated volunteers or killed in animal shelters because people watching those famous TV shows about those talented dogs want to buy one on the pet market, which mushrooms to fill the demand. The impulse buyers quickly find themselves with a serious dog whom they cannot satisfy with the work the Border Collie needs. And where is the labor of the hired shepherds and of the food-and-fiber producing sheep in this story? In how many ways do we inherit in the flesh the turbulent history of modern capitalism?

How to live ethically in these mortal, finite flows that are about heterogeneous relationship—and not about "man"—is an implicit question in Goldsworthy's art. His art is relentlessly attuned to specific human inhabitations of the land, but it is neither humanist nor naturalist art. It is the art of naturecultures. The relation is the smallest unit of analysis, and the relation is about significant otherness at every scale. That is the ethic, or perhaps better, mode of attention, with which we must approach the long cohabitings of people and dogs.

So, in *The Companion Species Manifesto*, I want to tell stories about relating in significant otherness, through which the partners come to be who we are in flesh and sign. The following shaggy dog stories about evolution, love, training, and kinds or breeds help me think about living well together with the host of species with whom human beings emerge on this planet at every scale of time, body, and space. The accounts I offer are idiosyncratic and indicative rather than systematic, tendentious more than judicious, and rooted in contingent foundations rather than clear and distinct premises. Dogs are my story here, but they are only one player in the large world of companion species. Parts don't add up to wholes in this mani-festo—or in life in naturecultures. Instead, I am looking for Marilyn Strathern's "partial connections," which are about the counter-intuitive geometries and incongruent translations necessary to getting on together, where the god-tricks of self certainty and deathless communion are not an option.

Evolution Stories

Everyone I know likes stories about the origin of dogs. Overstuffed with significance for their avid consumers, these stories are the stuff of high romance and sober science all mixed up together. Histories of human migrations and exchanges, the nature of technology, the meanings of wildness, and the relations of colonizers and colonized suffuse these stories. Matters like judging whether my dog loves me, sorting out scales of intelligence among animals and between animals and humans, and deciding whether humans are the masters or the duped can hang on the outcome of a sober scientific report. Evaluating the decadence or the progressiveness of breeds, judging whether dog behavior is the stuff of genes or rearing, adjudicating between the claims of old-fashioned anatomists and archaeologists or new-fangled molecular wizards, establishing origins in the New or Old World, figuring the ancestor of pooches as a noble hunting wolf persisting in modern endangered species or a cringing scavenger mirrored in mere village dogs, looking to one or many canine Eves surviving in their mitochondrial DNA or perhaps to a canine Adam through his Y-chromosome legacies—all these and more are understood to be at stake.

The day I wrote this section of *The Companion Species Manifesto*, news broke on the major networks from PBS to CNN about three papers in *Science* magazine on dog evolution and the history of domestication. Within minutes, numerous email lists in dogland were abuzz with discussion about the implications of the research. Website addresses flew across continents bringing the news to the cyborg world, while the merely literate followed the story in the daily papers of New York, Tokyo, Paris, or Johannesburg. What is going on in this florid consumption of scientific origin stories, and how can these accounts help me understand the relation that is companion species?

Explanations of primate, and especially hominid, evolution might be the most notorious cock-fighting arena in contemporary life sciences; but the field of canine evolution is hardly lacking in impressive dog fights among the human scientists and popular writers. No account of the appearance of dogs on earth goes unchallenged, and none goes unappropriated by its partisans. In both popular and professional dog worlds what is at stake is twofold: 1) the relation between what counts as nature and what counts as culture in Western discourse and its cousins, and 2) the correlated issue of who and what counts as an actor. These things matter for political, ethical, and emotional action in technoculture. A partisan in the world of dog evolutionary stories, I look for ways of getting co-evolution and co-constitution without strip-ping the story of its brutalities as well as multiform beauties.

Dogs are said to be the first domestic animals, displacing pigs for primal honors. Humanist techno-philiacs depict domestication as the paradigmatic act of masculine, single-parent, self-birthing, whereby man makes himself repetitively as he invents (creates) his tools. The domestic animal is the epoch-changing tool, realizing human intention in the flesh, in a dogsbody version of onanism. Man took the (free) wolf and made the (servant) dog and so made civilization possible. Mongrelized Hegel and Freud in the kennel? Let the dog stand for all domestic plant and animal species, subjected to human intent in stories of escalating progress or destruction, according to taste. Deep ecologists love to believe these stories in order to hate them in the name of Wilderness before the Fall into Culture, just as humanists believe them in order to fend off biological encroachments on culture.

These conventional accounts have been thoroughly reworked in recent years, when distributed everything is the name of the game all over, including in the kennel. Even though I know they are faddish, I like these metaplasmic, remodeled versions that give dogs (and other species) the first moves in domestication and then choreograph an unending dance of distributed and heterogeneous agencies. Besides being faddish, I think the newer stories have a better chance of being true, and they certainly have a better chance of teaching us to pay attention to significant otherness as something other than a reflection of one's intentions.

Studies of dog mitochondrial DNA as molecular clocks have indicated emergence of dogs earlier than previously thought possible. Work out of Carles Villá's and Robert Wayne's lab in 1997 argued for divergence of dogs from wolves as long as 150,000 years ago—that is, at the origin of *Homo sapiens sapiens*. That date, unsupported by fossil or archaeological evidence, has given way in subsequent DNA studies to somewhere from 50,000 to 15,000 years ago, with the scientists favoring the more recent date because it allows synthesis of all the available kinds of evidence. In that case, it looks like dogs emerged first somewhere in east Asia over a fairly brief time in a distributed pocket of events and then spread fast over the whole earth, going wherever humans went.

Many interpreters argue that the most likely scenario has wolf wannabe dogs first taking advantage of the calorie bonanzas provided by humans' waste dumps. By their opportunistic moves, those emergent dogs would be behaviorally and ultimately genetically adapted for reduced tolerance distances, less hair-trigger flight, puppy developmental timing with longer windows for cross-species socialization, and more confident parallel occupation of areas also occupied by dangerous humans. Studies of Russian fur foxes selected over many generations for differential tameness show many of the morphological and behavioral traits associated with domestication. These foxes might model the emergence of a kind of proto-"village dog," genetically close to wolves, as all dogs remain, but behaviorally quite different and receptive to human attempts to further the domestication process. Both by deliberate control of dogs' reproduction (e.g., killing unwanted puppies or feeding some bitches and not others) and by unintended but nonetheless potent consequences, humans could have contributed to shaping the many kinds of dogs that appeared early in the story. Human life ways changed significantly in association with dogs. Flexibility and opportunism are the name of the game for both species, who shape each other throughout the still ongoing story of co-evolution.

Scholars use versions of this story to question sharp divisions of nature and culture in order to shape a more generative discourse for technoculture. Darcy Morey, a canine paleobiologist and archaeologist, believes that the distinction between artificial and natural selection is empty because all the way down the story is about differential reproduction. Morey de-emphasizes intentions and foregrounds behavioral ecology. Ed Russell, an environmental historian, historian of technology, and science studies scholar, argues that the evolution of dog breeds is a chapter in the history of biotechnology. He emphasizes human agencies and regards organisms as engineered technologies, but in a way that has the dogs active, as well as in a way to foreground the ongoing co-evolution of human cultures and dogs. The science writer Stephen Budiansky insists that domestication in general, including the domestication of dogs, is a successful evolutionary strategy benefiting humans and their associated species alike. Examples can be multiplied.

These accounts taken together require re-evaluating the meanings of domestication and co-evolution. Domestication is an emergent process of co-habiting, involving agencies of many sorts and stories that do not lend themselves to yet one more version of the Fall or to an assured outcome for anybody. Co-habiting does not mean fuzzy and touchy-feely. Companion species are not companionate mates ready for early twentieth-century Greenwich Village anarchist discussions. Relationship is multiform, at stake, unfinished, consequential.

Co-evolution has to be defined more broadly than biologists habitually do. Certainly, the mutual adaptation of visible morphologies like flower sexual structures and the organs of their pollinating insects is co-evolution. But it is a mistake to see the alterations of dogs' bodies and minds as biological and the changes in human bodies and lives, for example in the emergence of herding or agricultural societies, as cultural, and so not about co-evolution. At the least, I suspect that human genomes contain a considerable molecular record of the pathogens of their companion species, including dogs. Immune systems are not a minor part of naturecultures; they determine where organisms, including people, can live and with whom. The history of the flu is unimaginable without the concept of the co-evolution of humans, pigs, fowl, and viruses.

But disease can't be the whole biosocial story. Some commentators think that even something as fundamental as the hypertrophied human biological capacity for speech emerged in consequence of associated dogs' taking on scent and sound alert jobs and so freeing the human face, throat, and brain for chat. I am skeptical of that account; but I am sure that once we reduce our own fight-or-flight reaction to emergent naturecultures, and stop seeing only biological reductionism or cultural uniqueness, both people and animals will look different.

I am heartened by recent ideas in ecological developmental biology, or "eco-devo" in the terms of developmental biologist and historian of science Scott Gilbert. Developmental triggers and timing are the key objects for this young science made possible by new molecular techniques and by discursive resources from many disciplines. Differential, context-specific plasticities are the rule, sometimes genetically assimilated and sometimes not. How organisms integrate environmental and genetic information at all levels, from the very small to the very large, determines what they become. There is no time or place at which genetics ends and environment begins, and genetic determinism is at best a local word for narrow ecological developmental plasticities.

The big, wide world is full of bumptious life. For example, Margaret McFall-Ngai has shown that the light-emitting organs of the squid *Euprymna scolopes* develop normally only if the embryo has been colonized by luminescent *Vibrio* bacteria. Similarly, human gut tissue cannot develop normally without colonization by its bacterial flora. The diversity of earth's animal forms emerged in the oceans' salty bacterial soup. All stages of the life histories of evolving animals had to adapt to eager bacteria colonizing them inside and out. Developmental patterns of complex life forms are likely to show the history of these adaptations, once scientists figure out how to look for the evidence. Earth's beings are prehensile, opportunistic, ready to yoke unlikely partners into something new, something symbiogenetic. Co-constitutive companion species and co-evolution are the rule, not the exception. These arguments are tropic for my manifesto, but flesh and figure are not far apart. Tropes are what make us want to look and need to listen for surprises that get us out of inherited boxes.

Love Stories

Commonly in the US, dogs are attributed with the capacity for "unconditional love." According to this belief, people, burdened with misrecognition, contradiction, and complexity in their relations with other humans, find solace in unconditional love from their dogs. In turn, people love their dogs as children. In my opinion, both of these beliefs are not only based on mistakes, if not lies, but also they are in themselves abusive—to dogs and to humans. A cursory glance shows that dogs and humans have always had a vast range of ways of relating. But even among the pet-keeping folk of contemporary consumer cultures, or maybe especially among these people, belief in "unconditional love" is pernicious. If the idea that man makes himself by realizing his intentions in his tools, such as domestic animals (dogs) and computers (cyborgs), is evidence of a neurosis that I call humanist technophiliac narcissism, then the superficially opposed idea that dogs restore human beings' souls by their unconditional love might be the neurosis of caninophiliac narcissism. Because I find the love of and between historically situated dogs and humans precious, dissenting from the discourse of unconditional love matters.

J.R. Ackerley's quirky masterpiece, *My Dog Tulip* (first privately printed in England in 1956), about a relationship between the writer and his "Alsatian" bitch in the 1940s and 1950s, gives me a way to think through my dissent. History flickers in the reader's peripheral vision from the start of this great love story. After two world wars, in one of those niggling examples of denial and substitution that allow us to go about our lives, a German Shepherd Dog in England was called an Alsatian. Tulip (Queenie, in real life) was the great love of Ackerley's life. An important novelist, famous homosexual, and splendid writer, Ackerley honored that love from the start by recognizing his impossible task—to wit, first, somehow to learn what *this* dog needed and desired and, second, to move heaven and earth to make sure she got it.

In Tulip, rescued from her first home, Ackerley hardly had his ideal love object. He also suspected he was not her idea of the loved one. The saga that followed was not about unconditional love, but about seeking to inhabit an inter-subjective world that is about meeting the other in all the fleshly detail of a mortal relationship. Barbara Smuts, the behavioral bioanthropologist who writes courageously about intersubjectivity and friendship with and among animals, would approve. No behavioral biologist, but attuned to the sexology of his culture, Ackerley comically and movingly sets out to find an adequate sexual partner for Tulip in her periodic heats.

The Dutch environmental feminist Barbara Noske, who also called our attention to the scandal of the meat-producing "animal-industrial complex," suggested thinking about animals as "other worlds" in a science fictional sense. In his unswerving dedication to his dog's significant otherness, Ackerley would have understood. Tulip mattered, and that changed them both. He also mattered to her, in ways that could only be read with the tripping proper to any semiotic practice, linguistic or not. The misrecognitions were as important as the fleeting moments of getting things right. Ackerley's story was full of the fleshly, meaning-making details of worldly, face-to-face love. Receiving unconditional love from another is a rarely excusable neurotic fantasy; striving to fulfill the messy conditions of being in love is quite another matter. The permanent search for knowledge of the intimate other, and the inevitable comic and tragic mistakes in that quest, commands my respect, whether the other is

Figure 2. Marco Harding and Willem DeKooning Caudill, a pet Great Pyrenees of Linda Weisser's breeding. Photo by the author.

animal or human, or indeed, inanimate. Ackerley's relationship with Tulip earned the name of love.

I have benefited from the mentoring of several life-long dog people. These people use the word love sparingly because they loathe how dogs get taken for cuddly, furry, child-like dependents. For example, Linda Weisser has been a breeder for more than thirty years of Great Pyrenees livestock guardian dogs, a health activist in the breed, and a teacher on all aspects of these dogs' care, behavior, history, and well being. Her sense of responsibility to the dogs and to the people who have them is stunning. Weisser emphasizes love of a *kind* of dog, of a breed, and talks about what needs to be done if people care about these dogs as a whole, and not just about one's own dogs. Without wincing, she recommends killing an aggressive rescue dog or any dog who has bitten a child; doing so could mean saving the reputation of the breed and the lives of other dogs, not to mention children. The "whole dog" for her is both a kind and an individual. This love leads her and others with very modest middle-class means to scientific and medical self-education, public action, mentoring, and major commitments of time and resources.

Weisser also talks about the special "dog of her heart"—a bitch who lived with her many years ago and who still stirs her. She writes in acid lyricism about a current dog who arrived at her house at eighteen months of age and snarled for three days, but who now accepts cookies from her nine-year-old granddaughter, allows the child to take away both food and toys, and tolerantly rules the household's younger bitches.

> I love this bitch beyond words. She is smart and proud and alpha, and if a snarl here and there is the price I pay for her in my life, so be it (Great Pyrenees Discussion List, 9/29/02).

Weisser plainly treasures these feelings and these relationships. She is quick to insist that at root her love is about

> the deep pleasure, even joy, of sharing life with a different being, one whose thoughts, feelings, reactions, and probably survival needs are different from ours. And somehow in order for all the species in this 'band' to thrive, we have to learn to understand and respect those things (Great Pyrenees Discussion List, 11/14/01).

To regard a dog as a furry child, even metaphorically, demeans dogs and children—and sets up children to be bitten and dogs to be killed. In 2001 Weisser had eleven dogs and five cats in residence. All of her adult life, she has owned, bred, and showed dogs; and she raised three human children and carried on a full civic, political life as a subtle left feminist. Sharing human language with her children, friends, and comrades is irreplaceable.

> While my dogs can love me (I think), I have never had an interesting political conversation with any of them. On the other hand, while my children can talk, they lack the true 'animal' sense that that allows me to touch, however briefly, the 'being' of another species so different from my own with all

the awe-inspiring reality that brings me (Great
Pyrenees Discussion List, 11/14/01).

Loving dogs the way Weisser means is not
incompatible with a pet relationship; indeed, pet relationships can and do frequently nurture this sort of
love. Being a pet seems to me to be a demanding job
for a dog, requiring self-control and canine emotional
and cognitive skills matching those of good working
dogs. Very many pets and pet people deserve respect.
Further, play between humans and pets, as well as
simply spending time peaceably hanging out together,
brings joy to all the participants. Surely that is one
important meaning of companion species.
Nonetheless, the status of pet puts a dog at special risk
in societies like the one I live in—the risk of abandon-
ment when human affection wanes, when people's
convenience takes precedence, or when the dog fails
to deliver on the fantasy of unconditional love.

Many of the serious dog people I have met
doing my research emphasize the importance to dogs
of jobs that leave them less vulnerable to human
consumerist whims. Weisser knows many livestock
people whose guardian dogs are respected for the
work they do. Some are loved and some are not, but
their value does not depend on an economy of affection. In particular, the dogs' value—and life— does
not depend on the humans' perception that the dogs
love them. Rather, the dog has to do his or her job,
and, as Weisser says, the rest is gravy.

Donald McCaig, the astute Border Collie
writer and sheepdog trialer, concurs. His novels, *Nop's*

Hope and *Nop's Trial*, are a superb introduction to potent relationships between working sheepdogs and their people. McCaig notes that working sheepdogs, as a category, fall "somewhere between 'livestock' and 'co-worker'" (Canine Genetics Discussion List, 11/30/00). A consequence of that status is that the dog's judgment may sometimes be better than the human's on the job. Respect and trust, not love, are the critical demands of a good working relationship between these dogs and humans. The dog's life depends more on skill—and on a rural economy that does not collapse—and less on a problematic fantasy.

In his zeal to foreground the need to breed, train, and work to sustain the precious herding abilities of the breed he best knows and most cares about, I think McCaig sometimes devalues and mis-describes both pet and sport performance relationships in dogland. I also suspect that his dealings with his dogs might properly be called love if that word were not so corrupted by our culture's infantilization of dogs and the refusal to honor difference. Dog naturecultures need his insistence on the functional dog preserved only by deliberate work-related practices, including breeding and economically viable jobs. We need Weisser's and McCaig's knowledge of the job of a kind of dog, the whole dog, the specificity of dogs. Otherwise, love kills, unconditionally, both kinds and individuals.

Training Stories

From "Notes of a Sports Writer's Daughter":

> *Marco, my godson, is Cayenne's god kid; she is his*
> *god dog. We are a fictive kin group in training. Perhaps*
> *our family coat of arms would take its motto from the*
> *Berkeley canine literary, politics, and arts magazine that*
> *is modeled after the* Barb; *namely, the* Bark, *whose*
> *masthead reads "dog is my co-pilot." When Cayenne was*
> *twelve weeks old and Marco six years old, my husband*
> *Rusten and I gave him puppy-training lessons for*
> *Christmas. With Cayenne in her crate in the car, I*
> *would pick Marco up from school on Tuesdays, drive to*
> *Burger King for a planet-sustaining health food dinner*
> *of burgers, coke, and fries, and then head to the Santa*
> *Cruz SPCA for our lesson. Like many of her breed,*
> *Cayenne was a smart and willing youngster, a natural*
> *to obedience games. Like many of his generation raised*
> *on high-speed visual special effects and automated cyborg*
> *toys, Marco was a bright and motivated trainer, a*
> *natural to control games.*
>
> *Cayenne learned cues fast, and so she quickly*
> *plopped her bum on the ground in response to a "sit"*
> *command. Besides, she practiced at home with me.*
> *Entranced, Marco at first treated her like a microchip-*
> *implanted truck for which he held the remote controls.*
> *He punched an imaginary button; his puppy magically*
> *fulfilled the intentions of his omnipotent, remote will.*
> *God was threatening to become our co-pilot. I, an obses-*
> *sive adult who came of age in the communes of the late*
> *1960s, was committed to ideals of inter-subjectivity and*
> *mutuality in all things, certainly including dog and boy*
> *training. The illusion of mutual attention and commu-*
> *nication would be better than nothing, but I really*

wanted more than that. Besides, here I was the only adult of either species present. Inter-subjectivity does not mean "equality," a literally deadly game in dogland; but it does mean paying attention to the conjoined dance of face-to-face significant otherness. In addition, control freak that I am, I got to call the shots, at least on Tuesday nights.

Marco was at the same time taking karate lessons, and he was profoundly in love with his karate master. This fine man understood the children's love of drama, ritual, and costume, as well as the mental-spiritual-bodily discipline of his marital art. "Respect" was the word and the act that Marco ecstatically told me about from his lessons. He swooned at the chance to collect his small, robed self into the prescribed posture and bow formally to his master or his partner before performing a form. Calming his turbulent first-grade self and meeting the eyes of his teacher or his partner in preparation for demanding, stylized action thrilled him. Hey, was I going to let an opportunity like that go unused in my pursuit of companion species flourishing?

"Marco," I said, "Cayenne is not a cyborg truck; she is your partner in a martial art called obedience. You are the older partner and the master here. You have learned how to perform respect with your body and your eyes. Your job is to teach the form to Cayenne. Until you can find a way to teach her how to collect her galloping puppy self calmly and to hold still and look you in the eyes, you cannot let her perform the 'sit' command." It would not be enough for her just to sit on cue and for him to "click and treat." That would be necessary, certainly, but the order was wrong. First, these two youngsters had to learn to notice each other. They had to be in the same game. It is my belief that Marco began to emerge as a dog trainer over the next six weeks. It is also my belief that as he learned to show her the corpo-

real posture of cross-species respect, she and he became significant others to each other.

Two years later out of the kitchen window I glimpsed Marco in the back yard doing twelve weave poles with Cayenne when nobody else was present. The weave poles are one of the most difficult agility objects to teach and to perform. I think Cayenne's and Marco's fast, beautiful weave poles were worthy of his karate master.

Positive Bondage

In 2002 the consummate agility competitor and teacher Susan Garrett authored a widely acclaimed training pamphlet called *Ruff Love*, published by the dog agility-oriented company, Clean Run Productions. Informed by behaviorist learning theory and the resultant popular positive training methods that have mushroomed in dogland in the last twenty years, the booklet instructs any dog person who wants a closer, more responsive training relationship with her or his dog. Problems like a dog's not coming when called or inappropriate aggression are surely in view; but, more, Garrett works to inculcate attitudes informed by biobehavioral research and to put effective tools in the hands of her agility students. She aims to show how to craft a relationship of energetic attention that would be rewarding to the dogs and the humans. Non-optional, spontaneous, oriented enthusiasm is to be the accomplishment of the previously most lax, distracted dog. I have the strong sense that Marco has been the subject of a similar pedagogy at his progressive elementary school. The rules are simple in principle and cunningly demanding in practice; to wit, mark the desired behavior with an instantaneous signal and then get a reward delivered within the time window appropriate to the species in question. The mantra of popular positive training, "click and treat," is only the tip of a vast post-"discipline and punish" iceberg.

Emphatically, as the back of Garrett's tract proclaims in a cartoon, positive does not mean permissive. Indeed, I have never read a dog-training manual more committed to near total control in the interests of fulfilling human intentions, in this case, peak performance in a demanding, dual species, competitive sport. That kind of performance can only come from a team that is highly motivated, not working under compulsion, but knowing the energy of each other and trusting the honesty and coherence of directional postures and responsive movements.

Garrett's method is exacting, philosophically and practically. The human partner must set things up so that the dog sees the clumsy biped as the source of all good things. Opportunities for the dog to get rewards in any other way must be eliminated as far as possible for the duration of the training program, typically a few months. The romantic might quail in the face of requirements to keep one's dog in a crate or tied to oneself by a loose leash. Forbidden to the pooch are the pleasures of romping at will with other dogs, rushing after a teasing squirrel, or clambering onto the couch—unless and until such pleasures are granted for exhibiting self control and responsiveness to the human's commands at a near 100% frequency. The human must keep detailed records of the *actual* correct response rate of the dog for each task, rather than tell tales about the heights of genius one's own dog must surely have reached. A dishonest human is in deep trouble in the world of ruff love.

The compensations for the dog are legion. Where else can a canine count on several focused training sessions a day, each designed so that the dog does not make mistakes, but instead gets rewarded by

the rapid delivery of treats, toys, and liberties, all care-
fully calibrated to evoke and sustain maximum motivation from the particular, individually known pupil?
Where else in dogland do training practices lead to a
dog who has learned to learn and who eagerly offers
novel "behaviors" that might become incorporated
into sports or living routines, instead of morosely
complying (or not) with poorly understood compul-
sions? Garrett directs the human to make careful lists
of what the dog actually likes; and she instructs people
how to play with their companions in a way *the dogs*
enjoy, instead of shutting dogs down by mechanical
human ball tosses or intimidating over-exuberance.
Besides all that, the human must actually enjoy playing
in doggishly appropriate ways, or they will be found
out. Each game in Garrett's book might be geared to
build success according to human goals, but unless the
game engages the dog, it is worthless.

In short, the major demand on the human is
precisely what most of us don't even know we don't
know how to do—to wit, how to see who the dogs are
and hear what they are telling us, not in bloodless
abstraction, but in one-on-one relationship, in otherness-in-connection.

There is no room for romanticism about the
wild heart of the natural dog or illusions of social
equality across the class Mammalia in Garrett's practice and pedagogy, but there is large space for disciplined attention and honest achievement.
Psychological and physical violence has no part in this
training drama; technologies of behavioral management have a staring role. I have made enough well

intentioned training mistakes—some of them painful to my dogs and some of them dangerous to people and other dogs, not to mention worthless for succeeding in agility—to pay attention to Garrett. Scientifically informed, empirically grounded practice matters; and learning theory is not empty cant, even if it is still a severely limited discourse and a rough instrument. Nonetheless, I am enough of a cultural critic to be unable to still the roaring ideologies of tough love in high-pressure, success-oriented, individualist America. Twentieth-century Taylorite principles of scientific management and the personnel management sciences of corporate America have found a safe crate around the postmodern agility field. I am enough of an historian of science to be unable to ignore the easily inflated, historically decontextualized, and overly generalized claims of method and expertise in positive training discourse.

Still, I lend my well-thumbed copy of *Ruff Love* to friends, and I keep my clicker and liver treats in my pocket. More to the point, Garrett makes me own up to the stunning capacity that dog people like me have to lie to ourselves about the conflicting fantasies we project onto our dogs in our inconsistent training and dishonest evaluations of what is actually happening. Her pedagogy of positive bondage makes a serious, historically specific kind of freedom for dogs possible; i.e., the freedom to live safely in multispecies, urban and sub-urban environments with very little physical restraint and no corporal punishment while getting to play a demanding sport with every evidence of self-actualizing motivation. In dogland, I am learning what my college teachers meant in their seminars on freedom and authority. I think my dogs rather like ruff tough love. Marco remains more skeptical.

Harsh Beauty

Vicki Hearne—the famous companion animal trainer, lover of maligned dogs like American Staffordshire Terriers and Airedales, and language philosopher—is at first glance the opposite of Susan Garrett. Hearne, who died in 2001, remains a sharp thorn in the paw for the adherents of positive training methods. To the horror of many professional trainers and ordinary dog folk, including myself, who have undergone a near-religious conversion from the military-style Koehler dog-training methods, not so fondly remembered for corrections like leash jerks and ear pinches, to the joys of rapidly delivering liver cookies under the approving eye of behaviorist learning theorists, Hearne did not turn from the old path and embrace the new. Her disdain for clicker training could be searing, exceeded only by her fierce opposition to animal rights discourse. I cringe under her ear pinching of my newfound training practices and rejoice in her alpha roll of animal rights ideologies. The coherence and power of Hearne's critique of both the clicker addicted and the rights besotted, however, command my respect and alert me to a kinship link. Hearne and Garrett are blood sisters under the skin.

The key to this close line breeding is their focused attention to what the dogs are telling them, and so demanding of them. Amazing grace, these thinkers attend to the dogs, in all these canines' situated complexity and particularity, as the unconditional demand of their relational practice. There is no doubt that behaviorist trainers and Hearne have important differences over methods, some of which could be resolved by empirical research and some of which are embedded in personal talent and cross-species charisma or in the incommensurable tacit knowledges of diverse communities of practice. Some of the differences also probably reside in human pigheadedness and canine opportunism. But "method" is not what matters most among companion species; "communication" across irreducible difference is what matters. Situated partial connection is what matters; the resultant dogs and humans emerge together in that game of cat's cradle. Respect is the name of the game. Good trainers practice the discipline of companion species relating under the sign of significant otherness.

Hearne's best-known book about communication between companion animals and human beings, *Adam's Task* (Random House, 1982), is ill titled. The book is about two-way conversation, not about naming. Adam had it easy in his categorical labor. He didn't have to worry about back-talk; and God, not a dog, made him who he was, in His own image, no less. To make matters harder, Hearne has to worry about conversation when human language isn't the medium, but not for reasons most linguists or language philosophers would give. Hearne likes trainers' using ordinary language in their work; that use turns out to be important to understanding what the dogs might be telling her, but not because the dogs are speaking furry humanese. She adamantly defends lots of so-called anthropomorphism, and no one more eloquently makes the case for the intention-laden, consciousness-

ascribing linguistic practices of circus trainers, eques-
trians, and dog obedience enthusiasts. All that philosophically suspect language is necessary to keep the
humans alert to the fact that somebody is at home in
the animals they work with.

Just *who* is at home must permanently be in
question. The recognition that one cannot *know* the
other or the self, but must ask in respect for all of time
who and what are emerging in relationship, is the key.
That is so for all true lovers, of whatever species.
Theologians describe the power of the "negative way
of knowing" God. Because Who/What Is is infinite, a
finite being, without idolatry, can only specify what is
not; i.e., not the projection of one's own self. Another
name for that kind of "negative" knowing is love. I
believe those theological considerations are powerful
for knowing dogs, especially for entering into a relationship, like training, worthy of the name of love.

I believe that all ethical relating, within or
between species, is knit from the silk-strong thread of
ongoing alertness to otherness-in-relation. We are not
one, and being depends on getting on together. The
obligation is to ask who are present and who are emergent. We know from recent research that dogs, even
kennel-raised puppies, do much better than generally
more brilliant wolves or human-like chimpanzees in
responding to human visual, indexical (pointing), and
tapping cues in a food-finding test. Dogs' survival in
species and individual time regularly depends on their
reading humans well. Would that we were as sure that
most humans respond at better than chance levels to
what dogs tell them. In fruitful contradiction, Hearne

thinks that the intention-ascribing idioms of experienced dog handlers can prevent the kind of literalist anthropomorphism that sees furry humans in animal bodies and measures their worth in scales of similarity to the rights-bearing, humanist subjects of Western philosophy and political theory.

Her resistance to literalist anthropomorphism and her commitment to significant otherness-in-connection fuel Hearne's arguments against animal rights discourse. Put another way, she is in love with the cross-species achievement made possible by the hierarchical discipline of companion animal training. Hearne finds excellence in action to be beautiful, hard, specific, and personal. She is against the abstract scales of comparison of mental functions or consciousness that rank organisms in a modernist great chain of being and assign privileges or guardianship accordingly. She is after specificity.

The outrageous equating of the killing of the Jews in Nazi Germany, the Holocaust, with the butcheries of the animal-industrial complex, made famous by the character Elizabeth Costello in J.M. Coetzee's novel *The Lives of Animals*, or the equating of the practices of human slavery with the domestication of animals make no sense in Hearne's framework. Atrocities, as well as precious achievements, deserve their own potent languages and ethical responses, including the assignment of priority in practice. Situated emergence of more livable worlds depends on that differential sensibility. Hearne is in love with the beauty of the ontological choreography when dogs and humans converse with skill, face-to-face. She is convinced that this is the choreography of "animal happiness," a title of another of her books.

In her famous blast in *Harper's* magazine in September 1991 titled "Horses, Hounds and Jeffersonian Happiness: What's Wrong with Animal Rights?" (available online with a new prologue at www.dogtrainingarts.com), Hearne asked what companion "animal happiness" might be. Her answer: the capacity for satisfaction that comes from striving, from work, from fulfillment of possibility. That sort of happiness comes from bringing out what is within; i.e., from what Hearne says animal trainers call "talent." Much companion animal talent can only come to fruition in the *relational* work of training. Following Aristotle, Hearne argues that this happiness is fundamentally about an ethics committed to "getting it right," to the satisfaction of achievement. A dog and handler discover happiness together in the labor of training. That is an example of emergent naturecultures.

This kind of happiness is about yearning for excellence and having the chance to try to reach it in terms recognizable to concrete beings, not to categorical abstractions. Not all animals are alike; their specificity—of kind and of individual—matter. The specificity of their happiness matters, and that is something that has to be brought to emergence. Hearne's translation of Aristotelian and Jeffersonian happiness is about human-animal flourishing as conjoined mortal beings. If conventional humanism is dead in post-cyborg and post-colonial worlds, Jeffersonian caninism might still deserve a hearing.

Bringing Thomas Jefferson into the kennel, Hearne believes that the origin of rights is in committed relationship, not in separate and pre-existing category identities. Therefore, in training, dogs obtain "rights" in specific humans. In relationship, dogs and humans construct "rights" in each other, such as the right to demand respect, attention, and response. Hearne described the sport of dog obedience as a place to increase the dog's power to claim rights against the human. Learning to obey one's dog honestly is the daunting task of the owner. Her language remaining relentlessly political and philosophical, Hearne asserts that in educating her dogs she "enfranchises" a relationship. The question turns out not to be what are animal rights, as if they existed preformed to be uncovered, but how may a human enter into a rights relationship with an animal? Such rights, rooted in reciprocal possession, turn out to be hard to dissolve; and the demands they make are life changing for all the partners.

Hearne's arguments about companion animal happiness, reciprocal possession, and the right to the pursuit of happiness are a far cry from the ascription of "slavery" to the state of all domestic animals, including "pets." Rather, for her the face-to-face relationships of companion species make something new and elegant possible; and that new thing is not human guardianship in place of ownership, even as it is also not property relations as conventionally understood. Hearne sees not only the humans, but also the dogs, as beings with a species-specific capacity for moral understanding and serious achievement. Possession—

property—is about reciprocity and rights of access. If I have a dog, my dog has a human; what that means concretely is at stake. Hearne remodels Jefferson's ideas of property and happiness even as she brings them into the worlds of tracking, hunting, obedience, and household manners.

Hearne's ideal of animal happiness and rights is also a far cry from the relief of suffering as the core human obligation to animals. Human obligation to companion animals is much more exacting than that, even as daunting as ongoing cruelty and indifference are in this domain too. The ethic of flourishing described by the environmental feminist Chris Cuomo is close to Hearne's approach. Something important comes into the world in the relational practice of training; all the participants are remodeled by it. Hearne loved language about language; she would have recognized metaplasm all the way down.

Apprenticed to Agility

From "Notes of a Sport's Writer's Daughter," *October, 1999:*

Dear Vicki Hearne,
    *Watching my Aussi-mix dog Roland with you
lurking inside my head last week made me remember
that such things are multidimensional and situational,
and describing a dog's temperament takes more precision
than I achieved. We go to an off-leash, cliff-enclosed
beach almost every day. There are two main classes of
dogs there: retrievers and metaretrievers. Roland is a
metaretriever. Roland will play ball with Rusten and me
once in a while (or anytime we couple the sport with a
liver cookie or two), but his heart's not in it. The activity
is not really self-rewarding to him, and his lack of style
shows it. But metaretrieving is another matter entirely.
The retrievers watch whoever is about to throw a ball or
stick as if their lives depended on the next few seconds.
The metaretrievers watch the retrievers with an
exquisite sensitivity to directional cues and microsecond
of spring. These meta dogs do not watch the ball or the
human; they watch the ruminant-surrogates-in-dog's-
clothing. Roland in meta-mode looks like an Aussie-
Border Collie mock up for a lesson in Platonism. His
forequarters are lowered, forelegs slightly apart with one
in front of the other in hair-trigger balance, his hackles
in mid-rise, his eyes focused, his whole body ready to
spring into hard, directed action. When the retrievers
sail out after the projectile, the metaretrievers move out
of their intense eye and stalk into heading, heeling,
bunching, and cutting their charges with joy and skill.
The good metaretrievers can even handle more than one
retriever at a time. The good retrievers can dodge the*

*metas and still make their catch in eye-amazing leaps—
or surges into the waves, if things have gone to sea.*

*Since we have no ducks or other surrogate sheep or
cattle on the beach, the retrievers have to do duty for the
metas. Some retriever people take exception to this
multitasking of their dogs (I can hardly blame them), so
those of us with metas try to distract our dogs once in a
while with some game they inevitably find much less
satisfying. I drew a mental Larson cartoon on Thursday
watching Roland, an ancient and arthritic Old English
Sheepdog, a lovely red tricolor Aussie, and a Border
Collie mix of some kind form an intense ring around a
shepherd-lab mix, a plethora of motley Goldens, and a
game pointer who hovered around a human who—
liberal individualist in Amerika to the end—was trying
to throw his stick to his dog only.*

*Figure 3. Cayenne Pepper leaping through the tire obstacle. Courtesy of
Tien Tran Photography.*

Correspondence with Gail Frazier, agility teacher, May 6, 2001:

Hi Gail,

Your pupils, Roland Dog and I, got 2 Qualifying scores in Standard Novice this weekend at the USDAA trial!

Our early morning Gamblers game on Saturday was a bad bet. And we were a disgrace to Agilitude in our Jumpers run, which finally happened at 6:30 p.m. Saturday evening. In our defense, after getting up at 4 a.m. on three hours sleep to get to Hayward for the trial, we were lucky to be standing by then, much less running and jumping. Both Roland and I ran totally separate jumpers courses, neither being the one the judge had prescribed. But our Standard runs Saturday and Sunday were both real pretty, and one earned us a 1st place ribbon. Roland's feet and my shoulders seemed born to dance together.

Cayenne and I head for Haute Dawgs in Dixon next Saturday for her first fun match. Wish us luck. There are so many ways to crash and burn on a course, but so far all of them have been fun, or at least instructive. Dissecting our respective runs Sunday afternoon in Hayward, one man and I were laughing at the cosmic arrogance of US culture (in this case, ourselves), in which we generally believe both that mistakes have causes and that we can know them. The gods are laughing.

The Game Story

Partly inspired by horse jumping events, the sport of dog agility first appeared at the Crufts dog show in London in February 1978 as entertainment during the break after the obedience championship and before the group judging. Also in agility's pedigree was police dog training, which began in London in 1946 and used obstacles like the high inclined A-frame that the Army had already adopted for its canine corps. Dog Working Trials, a demanding British competition that included three-foot-high bar jumps, six-foot-high panel jumps, and nine-foot broad jumps, added a third strand in agility's parentage. For early agility games, teeter-totters were scavenged from children's playgrounds; and coal mine ventilation shafts were put into service as tunnels. Men—many "guys who worked down the coal mines and wanted a bit of fun with their dogs," in the words of UK dog trainer and agility historian John Rogerson—were the original enthusiasts for these activities. Crufts and television, sponsored by Pedigree Pet Foods, assured that human gender and class would be as variable in the sport as the lineage of its equipment.

Immensely popular in Britain, agility spread around the world even faster than dogs had disbursed globally after their domestication. The United States Dog Agility Association (USDAA) was founded in 1986. By 2000, agility attracted thousands of addicted participants in hundreds of meets around the country. Typically a weekend event draws 300 or more dogs and handlers, and many teams trial more than once a month and train at least weekly. Agility flourishes in Europe, Canada, Latin America, Australia, and Japan. Brazil won the Fédération Cynologique Internationale's World Cup in 2002. The USDAA's Grand Prix event is televised, and its videotapes are devoured by agility enthusiasts for the new moves by the great dog-handler teams and new course layouts devised by devious judges. Week-long training camps attended by hundreds of students working with famous handler-instructors are held in several states.

Evidenced in the sport's glossy monthly magazine, *Clean Run*, agility is becoming ever more technically demanding. A course is made up of twenty or so obstacles like jumps, six-foot high A-frames, twelve weave poles in series, teeter-totters, and tunnels arranged in patterns by judges. Different games—called things like Snooker, Gamblers, Pairs, Jumpers with Weaves, Tunnelers, and Standard—involve different obstacle configurations and rules and require diverse strategies. Players see the courses for the first time the day of the event and get to walk through them for ten minutes or so to plan their runs. Dogs have not seen the course until they are actually running it. Humans give signals with voice and body; dogs navigate the obstacles at speed in the designated order. Scores depend on time and accuracy. A run typically takes a minute or less, and events are decided by fractions of seconds. Agility relies on fast-twitch muscles, skeletal and neural! Depending on the sponsoring organization, a dog-human team runs from two to eight events in a day. Recognition of obstacle patterns, knowledge of moves, skill on hard obstacles, and perfection of coordination and communication between dog and handler are the keys to good runs.

Agility can be expensive; travel, camping, entry fees, and training easily run to $2500 a year. To be good, teams need to practice several times a week and to be physically fit. The time commitment is not trivial for dogs or people. In the US, middle-aged, middle-class, white women dominate the sport numerically; the best players internationally are more various in gender, color, and age, but probably not class. All sorts of dogs play and win, but particular breeds— Border Collies, Shetland Sheepdogs, Jack Russell Terriers—excel in their jump height classes. The sport is strictly amateur, staffed and played by volunteers

Figure 4. Roland sailing over a bar jump. Courtesy of Tien Tran Photography.

and participants. Ann Leffler and Dair Gillespie, sociologists in Utah who study (and play) the sport, talk about agility in terms of "passionate avocations" that problematize the interface between public/private and work/leisure. I work to convince my sports writer father that agility should nudge football aside and take its rightful place on television with world-class tennis. Beyond the simple, personal fact of joy in time and work with my dogs, why do I care? Indeed, in a world full of so many urgent ecological and political crises, *how* can I care?

Love, commitment, and yearning for skill with another are not zero sum games. Acts of love like training in Vicki Hearne's sense breed acts of love like caring about and for other concatenated, emergent worlds. That is the core of my companion species manifesto. I experience agility as a particular good in itself and also as a way to become more worldly; i.e., more alert to the demands of significant otherness at all the scales that making more livable worlds demands. The devil here, as elsewhere, is in the details. Linkages are in the details. Someday I will write a big book called, if not *Birth of the Kennel* in honor of Foucault, then *Notes of a Sports Writer's Daughter* in honor of another of my progenitors, to argue for the myriad strands connecting dogs to the many worlds we need to make flourish. Here, I can only suggest. To do that, I will work tropically by appealing to three phrases that Gail Frazier, my agility teacher, regularly uses with her students: "you left your dog"; "your dog doesn't trust you"; and "trust your dog."

These three phrases return us to Marco's story, Garrett's positive bondage, and Hearne's harsh beauty. A good agility teacher, like mine, can show her students exactly where they left their dogs and exactly what gestures, actions, and attitudes block trust. It's all quite literal. At first, the moves seem small, insignificant; the timing too demanding, too hard; the consistency too strict, the teacher too demanding. Then, dog and human figure out, if only for a minute, how to get on together, how to move with sheer joy and skill over a hard course, how to communicate, how to be honest. The goal is the oxymoron of disciplined spontaneity. Both dog and handler have to be able to take the initiative and to respond obediently to the other. The task is to become coherent enough in an incoherent world to engage in a joint dance of being that breeds respect and response in the flesh, in the run, on the course. And then to remember how to live like that at every scale, with all the partners.

Breed Stories

So far this manifesto has foregrounded two sorts of time-space scales co-constituted by human, animal, and inanimate agencies: 1) evolutionary time at the level of the planet earth and its naturalcultural species, and 2) face-to-face time at the scale of mortal bodies and individual lifetimes. Evolutionary stories attempted to calm my political people's fears of biological reductionism and, with my colleague in science studies, Bruno Latour, interest them in the much more lively ventures of naturecultures. Love and training stories tried to honor the world in its irreducible, personal detail. At every repetition, my manifesto works fractally, re-inscribing similar shapes of attention, listening, and respect.

It is time to sound tones on another scale, namely, historical time on the scale of decades, centuries, populations, regions, and nations. Here, I borrow from Katie King's work on feminism and writing technologies, where she asks how to recognize emergent forms of consciousness, including methods of analysis, implicated in globalization processes. She writes about distributed agencies, "layers of locals and globals," and political futures yet to be actualized. Dog people need to learn how to inherit difficult histories in order to shape more vital multi-species futures. Attention to layered and distributed complexity helps me to avoid both pessimistic determinism and romantic idealism. Dogland turns out to be built from layers of locals and globals.

I need feminist anthropologist Anna Tsing to think about scale-making in dogland. She interrogated what gets to count as the "global" in transnational financial wheeling and dealing in contemporary Indonesia. She saw not pre-existing entities already in the shapes and scales of frontiers, centers, locals, or globals, but instead "scale–making" of world-making kinds, in which re-opening what seemed closed remains possible.

Finally, I translate—literally, move over to dogland—Neferti Tadiar's understanding of experience as living historical labor, through which subjects can be structurally situated in systems of power without reducing them to raw material for the Big Actors like Capitalism and Imperialism. She might forgive me for including dogs among those subjects, and she would give me the human-dog dyad at least provisionally. Let us see if telling histories of two divergent kinds of dogs—livestock guardian dogs (LGDs) and herders— and of institutionalized breeds emergent from those kinds—Great Pyrenees and Australian Shepherds—as well as of dogs of no fixed breed or kind, can help shape a potent worldly consciousness in solidarity with my feminist, anti-racist, queer, and socialist comrades; that is, with the imagined community that can only be known through the negative way of naming, like all the ultimate hopes.

In that negative way, I tell declarative stories trippingly. There are myriad origin and behavior stories about breeds and kinds of dogs, but not all narratives are born equal. My mentors in dogland taught me their breed histories, which I think honor

both lay and scientific documentary, oral, experi-
mental, and experiential evidence. The following
stories are composites that, interpellating me into
their structures, show something important about
companion species living in naturecultures.

Great Pyrenees

Guardian dogs associated with sheep- and goat-herding peoples go back thousands of years and cover wide swaths of Africa, Europe, and Asia. Local and long-range migrations of millions of grazers, shepherds, and dogs to and from markets and to and from winter and summer pastures—from the Atlas Mountains of north Africa, crossing Portugal and Spain, throughout the Pyrenean mountains, across southern Europe, over into Turkey, into eastern Europe, across Eurasia, and through Tibet and into China's Gobi Desert—have literally carved deep tracks into soil and rock. In their rich book, *Dogs* (Scribner, 2001), Raymond and Lorna Coppinger compare these tracks to the carving of glaciers. Regional livestock guardian dogs developed into distinct kinds in both appearance and attitude, but sexual communication always linked adjacent or traveling populations. The dogs that developed in higher, more northern, colder climates are bigger than those that took shape in Mediterranean or desert ecologies. The Spanish, English, and other Europeans brought their big mastiff-type and little shepherd-type dogs to the Americas in that massive gene exchange known as the conquest. Such interconnecting but far from randomly mixed populations are ecological and genetic population biologists' dreams or nightmares, depending on that hard thing called history.

Post mid-nineteenth-century kennel club breeds of LGDs with closed stud books derive from varying numbers of individuals collected from regional kinds, such as the Pyrenean Mastiff in the Basque area of Spain, the Great Pyrenees in Basque regions of France and Spain, the Maremma in Italy, Kuvasz in Hungary, and Anatolian Sheepdog in Turkey. The controversies about the genetic health and functional significance of these closed "island" populations called breeds rage in dogland. A breed club is partly analogous to a managing association for endangered species, for which population bottlenecks and disruption of past genetic natural and artificial selection systems require sustained, organized action.

Traditionally, LGDs protect flocks from bears, wolves, thieves, and strange dogs. LGDs often work with herding dogs in the same flocks, but the canines' jobs are different and their interactions limited. Regionally distinct, smallish herding dogs were everywhere, including hoards of collie types we will hear more about when I turn to Australian Shepherds. Peasant-shepherds across the huge land mass and time span of herding economies applied strong functional standards to their dogs that directly affected survival and breeding opportunities and shaped type. Ecological conditions also shaped the dogs and sheep independently of human intentions. Meanwhile, the dogs, employing different criteria, surely exercised their own sexual proclivities with their neighbors when they had the chance.

Guardian dogs do not herd sheep; they protect them from predators, mainly by patrolling boundaries and energetically barking to warn off strangers. They will attack and even kill intruders who insist, but their ability to calibrate their aggression to the level of the threat is legendary. They also perfect a repertoire of distinct barks for kinds and levels of alerts. Livestock guardian dogs tend to have low prey drive; and little of their puppy play involves chase, gather, head, heel, and grab-bite games. If they start to play like that with livestock or each other, the shepherd dissuades them. Those not dissuaded don't stay in the LGD gene pool. Working LGDs show the ropes to youngsters; lacking that, a knowledgeable human must help a lone puppy or older dog learn to be a good guardian—or, conversely, ignorantly set the neophyte up for failure.

Livestock guardian dogs tend to make lousy retrievers, and their biosocial predilections and upbringing conspire to deafen most to the siren songs of higher obedience competition. But they are capable of impressive independent decision-making in a complex historical ecology. Stories about LGDs helping ewes give birth and licking the newborn lamb clean dramatize the dogs' capacity to bond with their charges. A livestock guardian dog, like a Great Pyrenees, might pass the day lounging among the sheep and the night patrolling, happily alert for trouble.

LGDs and herders tend to learn things with differential ease or difficulty. Neither kind of dog can really be taught to do their core jobs, much less the other dog's work. Dogs' functional behavior and attitudes can and must be directed and encouraged—trained, in that sense—but a dog with little joy in chasing and gathering and no deep interest in working with a human cannot be shown how to herd skillfully. Herders have strong prey drive from puppy-hood. Choreographed with human herders and their herbivores, controlled components of that predation pattern, minus the kill and dissect parts, are precisely what herding is. Similarly, a dog with little passion for territory, anemic suspicion of intruders, and dim pleasure in social bonding cannot be shown from scratch how to think well about these things, even with the world's biggest clicker.

Figure 5. Mary Crane in July, 1967, at the Great Pyrenees Club of America National Specialty Show in Santa Barbara, CA. The dog next to Mrs. Crane is Armand (Ch. Los Pyrtos Armand of Pyr Oaks), who won the stud dog class that day. Next to him are his two daughters, Impy, who went Reserve Winners bitch, and Drifty, who was Best of Opposite Sex. Linda Weisser is the young woman with Drifty, who died without offspring. Weisser's "dog of my heart," Impy has descendants in almost all US west coast kennels. Through a son, Armand is behind Catherine de la Cruz's working ranch stock. Photo by courtesy of L. Weisser and C. de la Cruz.

Guarding flocks in Europe since at least Roman times, large white guardian dogs appear in French records over the centuries. In 1885-86, Pyrenean Mountain Dogs were registered with the Kennel Club in London. In 1909, the first Pyrs were brought to England for breeding. In his monumental 1897 encyclopedia *Les races des chiens*, Conte Henri de Bylandt dedicated several pages to describing Pyrenean guardian dogs. Forming rival clubs at Lourdes and Argeles, in 1907 two groups of French fanciers bought mountain dogs that they regarded as worthy and "purebred." Complete with the romantic idealization of peasant-shepherds and their animals characteristic of capitalist modernization and class formations that make such life ways nearly impossible, discourses of pure blood and nobility haunt modern breeds like the undead.

World War I destroyed both French clubs and most of the dogs. Working guardian dogs in the mountains were ravaged by war and depression, but they had already lost most of their jobs by the turn of the nineteenth century due to the extirpation of bears and wolves. Pyrs had become more likely to hang out as village dogs and be sold to tourists and collectors than put to work guarding flocks. In 1927, the diplomat, show judge, breeder, and native of the Pyrenees, Bernard Senac-Lagrange joined the few remaining fanciers to found the Réunion des Amateurs de Chiens Pyreneans and write the description that remains the foundation for current standards.

In the 1930s, serious collecting by two wealthy women, Mary Crane from Massachusetts (Basquaerie

Kennels), and Mme. Jeanne Harper Trois Fontaine, born in Belgium but married in England (de Fontenay Kennel), brought many dogs out of France. The American Kennel Club recognized Great Pyrenees in 1933. World War II took another toll on the remaining LGDs in the Pyrenees and wiped out most of the French and Northern European registered kennel dogs. Asking how closely related they were and which left offspring, Pyr historians have tried to figure out how many dogs Mary Crane, Mme. Harper, and a few others bought, both from villagers and from fanciers. As few as thirty dogs, many related to each other, contributed in any continuing way to the gene pool of Pyrs in the US. By the end of World War II, the only sizable Pyr populations in the world were in the UK and the US, although the breed later recovered in France and northern Europe, with some exchange between US and European breeders. The continuing existence of the dogs was largely due to the passionate show enthusiasts and breeders of the dog fancy. From 1931 when Mary Crane started collecting until the 1970s, very few US Pyrs worked as livestock guardian dogs.

That changed with emerging approaches to predator control in the western United States in the early 1970s. Loose dogs killed lots of sheep. Coyotes also killed livestock; and they were ferociously poisoned, trapped, and shot by ranchers. Catherine de la Cruz—who got her first Pyr show bitch, Belle, in 1967 and was mentored in Great Pyrenees by Ruth Rhoades, the "mother superior" in the breed in California who also taught Linda Weisser—lived on a dairy ranch in Sonoma County. This middle-class, west-coast, Pyr scene marks important differences in the breed's culture and future.

In 1972, a UC-Davis scientist telephoned de la Cruz's mother to talk about predator losses. The agribusiness research university and the US Department of Agriculture were beginning to take non-toxic methods of predator control seriously. Environmental and animal rights activists were making their voices heard in public consciousness and national policy, including Federal restrictions on using poisons to kill predators. De la Cruz's Belle hung out with the dairy cows between dog shows; that ranch never had any trouble with predators. De la Cruz relates that "the light went on in her head." The Great Pyrenees Standard describes the dogs guarding

Figure 6. Great Pyrenees puppy learning the job. Photo courtesy of Linda Weisser.

flocks from bears and wolves, although that was more the symbolic narrative of show fanciers than descriptions of what any of them had seen. Whatever else it also does, the written standard in an institutionalized breed is about ideal type and origin narrative. In her own origin story, de la Cruz tells that she began to think that the Pyrs she knew might be able to guard sheep and cows from dogs and coyotes.

De la Cruz gave some puppies to northern California sheep people she knew. From there, she and a few other Pyr breeders, including Weisser, placed dogs (including some adults) on ranches and tried to figure out how to help the dogs become effective Predator Control Dogs, as they were called then. The dairy farm was converted to sheep ranching, and de la Cruz became part of the woolgrowers association. In the late 1970s, she met Margaret Hoffman, a woman active in the woolgrowers group who wanted dogs to repel coyotes. Hoffman got Sno-Bear from de la Cruz, bred more dogs, and placed 100% of them in working homes. In an interview with me in November 2002, de la Cruz talks about "making every possible mistake," experimenting with socializing and caring for working dogs, staying in close touch with the ranchers, and cooperating with UC-Davis and Department of Agriculture people in research and placement.

In the 1980s, Linda Weisser and Evelyn Stuart, part of the Great Pyrenees Club of America committee to revise the standard, made sure that the functional, working dogs were prominently in view. By the 1980s, de la Cruz, still showing dogs in conformation, was placing working Pyrs around the country. A few of the dogs came in from the pastures, got their baths, won championships, and went right back to work. The "dual purpose dog" became a moral and practical ideal in Pyr breeding and breed education. Mentoring to achieve this ideal involves all kinds of labor—and labor-intensive—practices, including managing high-quality Internet listservs like the Livestock Guardian Dog Discussion List and the stockguard topic section of the Great Pyrenees Discussion List. Lay expertise, volunteer labor, and collaborating communities of practice are crucial. Not least, every working Pyr in the US comes through a pet and show home history of more than four decades. Companion species and emergent naturecultures appear everywhere I look.

Beginning in the mid-1970s, first Jeffrey Green and then also Roger Woodruff of the US Sheep Experiment Station of the US Department of Agriculture (USDA) in Dubois, Idaho, are key actors in this story. Their first guardian dog was a Komondor (Hungary), and they then worked with Akbash (Turkey) and Pyrs. My Pyr informants discuss these men with tremendous respect. Urging ranchers to try out the guardian dogs, the USDA men solicited breeders' help and treated them as colleagues. For example, Woodruff and Green gave a special seminar on LGDs at the Great Pyrenees Club of America National Specialty show in Sacramento in 1984. Another piece of the story of the re-emergence of working LGDs in North America is Hal Black's early-1980s study of Navajo sheep herding practices with their effective mongrel dogs to glean lessons for other ranchers.

Rancher re-education was a big part of the USDA project, and Pyr people engaged that process energetically. Steeped in the modernization ideologies of the science-based, land-grant universities and agribusiness, ranchers tended to see dogs as old fashioned and commercial poisons as progressive and profitable. Dogs are not a quick fix; they require changed labor practices and investments of time and money. Working with ranchers to effect change has been modestly successful.

In 1987 and 1988, the USDA project bought about 100 guardian dog puppies from around the US, most of them Pyrs. The USDA scientists agreed to the breed club people's insistence on spaying and neutering the dogs placed through the project, which kept at least those dogs out of puppy mill production and other breeding practices that the club people believe harmful to the dogs' well being and genetic health. To reduce the risk of hip dysplasia in the working dogs, all of the parents of the pups had their hips checked by X-rays. By the late 1980s, surveys indicated that over 80% of ranchers found their guardian dogs—especially their Great Pyrenees—to be an economic asset. By 2002, a few thousand LGDs are in charge of the protection of sheep, llamas, cattle, goats, and ostriches throughout the US.

Raymond and Lorna Coppinger and their associates at Hampshire College's New England Farm Center, beginning with Anatolian Shepherds brought from Turkey in the late 1970s, also did research and placed hundreds of LGDs on American farms and ranches. Raymond Coppinger has a PhD in the tradition of Niko Tinbergen's ethology legacy at Oxford University, and the Coppingers also have a serious history in racing sled dogs. The Coppingers have always been more in the public eye and better known by scientists, other than those directly involved in LGD work, than the lay breeders whom I emphasize in my story. The Coppingers dissent on many points from the view of guardian dogs held by my Pyr people. The Hampshire College project did not sterilize dogs they placed. Believing that the social environment during maturation was the only crucial variable in shaping an effective stock guardian, they did not generally take breed distinctions seriously. The Hampshire project placed younger puppies, taught a different view of biosocial development and genetic behavioral predilections, and handled the mentoring of people and dogs differently.

Most Pyr people did not cooperate with the Coppingers, and animosity dates from the start. Effectively, the Coppingers had little access to Great Pyrenees, where the breed club ethic was strong. I cannot evaluate the differences here, and the reader can find the Coppingers' views in *Dogs*. However, in that book, there is no mention of the Pyr people, including that they were placing livestock guardian dogs and cooperating with Jeff Green and Roger Woodruff from the start. Readers will also not learn, as they could in a 1990 USDA publication, that in a 1986 survey of 400 people, involving 763 dogs, conducted by the University of Idaho, Great Pyrenees made up 57% of the population. Pyrs and Komodors, another breed whose people did not contribute to the Hampshire

Project, accounted for 75% of the working LGDs in the study. That study and others show that Pyrs tend to get the highest marks of any breed for job success. That includes biting fewer people and injuring fewer livestock. In a study of yearling dogs involving 59 Pyrs and 26 Anatolian Shepherds, 83% of Pyrs got a score of "good" compared to 26% of the Anatolians.

The introduction, from blasted peasant-shepherd economies, of Basque Pyrenean mountain dogs, who were nurtured in the purebred dog fancy, onto the ranches of the US west to protect Anglo ranchers' xenobiological cattle and sheep on the grasslands habitat (where few native grasses survive) of buffalo once hunted by Plains Indians riding Spanish horses—along with the study of contemporary reservation Navajo sheep-herding cultures deriving from Spanish conquest and missionization—ought to offer enough historical irony for any companion species manifesto. But there is more. Two efforts to bring back extirpated predator species rehabilitated from the status of vermin to natural wildlife and tourist attraction, one in the Pyrenean mountains and one in the national parks of the American west, will lead us further into the web.

The Endangered Species Act in the US gives the Department of the Interior jurisdiction over re-introduction of the gray wolf to parts of its previous range, such as Yellowstone National Park, where four-teen Canadian wolves were released in 1995 in the midst of the country's largest elk and buffalo populations. Migrating Canadian wolves began showing up in Montana on their own initiative. In 1995-96, fifty-two more wolves were released in Idaho and Wyoming.

About 700 wolves live in the northern Rocky Mountains in 2002. By and large, ranchers remain unreconciled, even though they get full monetary compensation for stock losses and stock-killing wolves are removed or killed by the Fish and Wildlife Service of the Department of the Interior. According to Jim Robbins' *New York Times* report on December 17, 2002 (p. D3), 20% of the closely managed wolves wear electronic monitoring collars. Coyote numbers are down; wolves kill them. Elk numbers are down. That makes hunters unhappy but pleases ecologists worried about damage from herbivores deprived of their predators. Tourists—and the businesses that serve them—are very happy. More than 100,000 tourist wolf sightings have been logged on car safaris in the Lamar Valley in Wyoming. No tourists have been killed, but national figures in 2002 showed that 200 cattle, 500 sheep, 7 llamas, 1 horse, and 43 dogs have been. Who were those 43 dogs?

Some of them were ill-prepared Great Pyrenees. The Department of the Interior put wolves in Yellowstone National Park against ranchers' wishes; without coordination with the Department of Agriculture LGD people in Idaho; and without, I suspect, even imaging talking to knowledgeable Pyr breeders, who are also late middle-aged white women who show their gorgeous dogs in conformation. Interior and Agriculture are worlds apart in technoscientific culture. The wolves spilled out of park boundaries. Wolves, livestock, and dogs all got killed, maybe needlessly. Wildlife officials have killed over 125 errant wolves; ranchers have illegally shot at least dozens more. Wildlife conservationists, tourists, ranchers, bureaucrats, and communities got polarized, maybe needlessly. Better companion species relations needed to be formed all around, from the start, among the humans and the non-humans.

Dogs are social and territorial; wolves are social and territorial. Experienced LGDs in large enough established groups might be able to deter northern gray wolves from munching on livestock. But bringing Pyrs to the scene after the wolves have set up shop or using too few and inexperienced dogs are sure recipes for disaster for both canid species and for weaving together wildlife and ranching ethics. The group Defenders of Wildlife has bought Pyrs for ranchers experiencing losses to wolves; the wolves seem actively drawn to and kill the dogs as intruding competitors on wolf real estate. Practices that might have led wolves to respect organized dogs were not in place; it might be too late for LGDs to be effective actors in wolf flour-ishing and rancher-conservationist alliances. Maybe the wolves will control the coyotes while the Pyrs are protected indoors at night.

Meanwhile, restoration ecology has its European flavors. In the Pyrenees, the French govern-ment has introduced European Brown Bears from Slovakia, where the post-communist tourist industry makes a tidy sum promoting bear watching, to fill the empty niche left by killing the previous ursine resi-dents. French Pyr fanciers, such as the goat farmer, Benoit Cockenpot of du Pic de Viscos kennel, work to get the dogs back in the mountains telling the Slovakian bears the proper postmodern order of things.

The French Pyr fanciers are learning about working LGDs from their US colleagues. The French government offers farmers a free guardian dog. But insurance reimburses farmers for animals lost to predators, and that is turning out to be more attractive than daily taking care of dogs. Guardian dogs have a harder time competing with the insurance apparatus than repelling bears.

Away from multi-species conservation and farm politics, Pyrs never stopped excelling as show dogs and pets. However, the breed's numerical expansion as both workers and pets has meant considerable escape from the breed club's control, much less the control of a viable peasant-shepherd economy, into the hells and limbos of commercial puppy production and backyard breeding. Indifference to health; ignorance of behavior, socialization, and training; and cruel conditions are all too frequent. Within the breed clubs, controversy reigns over what constitutes responsible breeding, especially when the hard-to-digest topics of genetic diversity and population genetics in purebred dogs are on the menu. Overuse of popular sires, secrecy about dogs' problems, and lusting for show ring championships at the expense of other values are practices known to imperil dogs. Too many people still do it. Love of dogs forbids it, and I have met many of these lovers in my research. These are the people who get dirty and knowledgeable in all the worlds where their dogs live—on farms, in labs, at shows, in homes, and wherever else. I want their love to flourish; that is one reason I write.

Australian Shepherds

The herding breed known in the United States as the Australian Shepherd, or Aussies, raises just as many complexities as Great Pyrenees; I will sketch only a few. My point is simple: Knowing and living with these dogs means inheriting all of the conditions of their possibility, all of what makes relating with these beings actual, all of the prehensions that constitute companion species. To be in love means to be worldly, to be in connection with significant otherness and signifying others, on many scales, in layers of locals and globals, in ramifying webs. I want to know how to live with the histories I am coming to know.

If anything is certain about Australian Shepherd origins, it is that no one knows how the

Figure 7. Beret's Dogon Grit winning High in Sheep at the 2002 Australian Shepherd Club of America National Stock Dog Finals, Bakersfield, CA. Courtesy of Glo Photo and Gayle Oxford.

name came about, and no one knows all of the kinds of dogs tied in the ancestry of these talented herders. Perhaps the surest thing is that the dogs should be called the United States Western Ranch Dog. Not "American," but "United States." Let me explain why that matters, especially since most (but far from all) of the ancestors are probably varieties of collie types that emigrated with their people from the British Isles to the east coast of North America from early colonial times on. The California Gold Rush and the after-math of the Civil War are the keys to my regional national story. These epic events made the American west into part of the United States. I don't want to inherit these violent histories, as Cayenne, Roland, and I run our agility courses and conduct our oral affairs; that's why I have to tell them. Companion species cannot afford evolutionary, personal, or historical amnesia. Amnesia will corrupt sign and flesh and make love petty. If I tell the story of the Gold Rush and the Civil War, then maybe I can remember the other stories about the dogs and their people—stories about immigration, indigenous worlds, work, hope, love, play, and the possibility of co-habitation through reconsidering sovereignty and ecological developmental naturecultures.

Romantic origin stories about Aussies have late nineteenth- and early twentieth-century Basque herders bringing their little blue merle dogs with them in steerage as they headed, via sojourn in Australia herding Merino sheep from Spain, for the ranches of California and Nevada to tend the sheep of a timeless pastoral west. "In steerage" gives the game away; working class men in steerage were in no position to bring their dogs, to Australia or to California. Besides, the Basques who emigrated to Australia did not become herders, but sugar cane workers; and they did not go down under until the twentieth century. Not necessarily shepherds before, the Basques came to California, sometimes via South America and Mexico, in the nineteenth century with the millions lusting for gold and ended up herding sheep to feed other disappointed miners. The Basques also established great restaurants, heavy on lamb dishes, in Nevada on what became the interstate highway system after World War II. The Basques got their sheep dogs from among local working herding dogs, who were a mixed lot, to say the least.

Spanish missions favored sheep ranching to civilize the Indians, but in her online version of Aussie history (www.glassportal.com/herding/shepherd.htm), Linda Rorem notes that by the 1840s the number of sheep (not to mention Native people) in the far west had greatly declined. Discovery of gold radically and permanently changed the food economy, politics, and ecology of the region. Large sheep flocks were transported by sailing them from the east coast around the Horn, driving them overland from the mid-west and New Mexico, and shipping them from that "nearby" white settler colony with a colonial pastoral economy, Australia. Many of these sheep were Merinos, originally of Spanish origin, but coming to Australia through Germany, via a gift from Spain's king to Saxony, which developed a thriving colonial export trade in sheep.

What the Gold Rush began, the aftermath of the Civil War finished, with its vast influx of Anglo (and some African-American) settlers to the west and the military destruction and containment of Native Americans and consolidations of expropriated land from Mexicans, Californios, and Indians.

All of these movements of sheep also meant movements of their herding dogs. These were not the guardian dogs of the old Eurasian pastoral economies, with their established market routes, seasonal pasturages, and local bears and wolves—which were, nonetheless, heavily depleted. The settler colonies in Australia and the US adopted an even more aggressive attitude to natural predators—building fences around most of Queensland to keep out dingoes and trapping, poisoning, and shooting anything with serious canine teeth that moved upon the land in the US west. Guardian dogs did not appear in the US western sheep economy until after these tactics became illegal in the queer times of effective environmental movements.

The herding dogs accompanying the immigrant sheep from both the east coast and Australia were mainly of the old working collie/shepherd types. These were strong, multi-purpose dogs with a "loose eye" and upstanding working posture—rather than with a sheep trial-selected, Border-Collie hard eye and crouch—from which several kennel-club breeds derive. Among the dogs coming to the US west from Australia were the frequently merle-colored "German Coulies," who look a lot like modern Australian Shepherds. These were British-derived, all-purpose herding "collies," called "German" because German settlers lived in an area of Australia where these dogs were common. Dogs that look like contemporary Aussies might have gotten their name early from being associated with flocks arriving on boats from down under, whether or not they came on those ships. Or, associated with later immigrant dogs, these types might have started being called "Australian Shepherds" as late as World War I. Written records are scarce. And there wasn't a "purebred" in sight for a long time.

There were, however, identifiable lines in California, Washington, Oregon, Colorado, and Arizona developing by the 1940s that became registered Australian Shepherds, beginning in 1956. Registration was not common until the mid- to late-1970s. The range of types was still wide, and styles of dogs were associated with particular families and ranches. Curiously, a rodeo performer from Idaho named Jay Sisler is part of the story of molding a kind of dog into a contemporary breed, complete with its clubs and politics. Over twenty years, Sisler's "blue dogs" were a popular rodeo trick show. He knew the parents of most of these dogs, but that is as deep as genealogy got in the beginning. Sisler got his dogs from various ranchers, several of whose Aussies became foundation stock of the breed. Among the identified 1371 dogs out of 2046 ancestors in her ten-generation pedigree, I count seven Sisler dogs in my Cayenne's family. (Many with names like "Redding Ranch Dog" and "Blue Dog," 6170 out of over a million ancestors are known in her twenty-generation tree; that leaves a few gaps.)

An amazing trainer of the type Vicki Hearne would have loved, Sisler considered Keno, whom he got around 1945, to be his first really good dog. Keno contributed offspring to what became the breed; but the Sisler dog who made the biggest impact (percentage ancestry) to the current population of Aussies was John, a dog with unknown antecedents who wandered one day onto the Sisler ranch and into written pedigrees. There are many such stories of foundation dogs. They could all be microcosms for thinking about companion species and the invention of tradition in the flesh, as well as the text.

The Aussie parent club, the Australian Shepherd Club of America (ASCA), was founded in Tucson by a small group of enthusiasts in 1957. ASCA wrote a preliminary standard in 1961 and a firm one in 1977 and got its own breed club registry going in 1971. Organized in 1969, the ASCA Stock Dog Committee organized herding trials and titles; and working ranch dogs began their considerable re-education for the trial ring. Conformation competitions and other events became popular, and sizable numbers of Aussie people saw AKC affiliation as the next step. Other Aussie people saw AKC recognition as the road to perdition for any working breed. The pro-AKC people broke away to found their own club, the United States Australian Shepherd Association (USASA), which got full AKC recognition in 1993.

All of the biosocial apparatus of modern breeds emerged—including savvy lay health and genetics activists, scientists researching illnesses common in the breed and perhaps establishing companies to market resultant vet biomedical products, Aussie-themed small businesses, performers passionate about the dogs in agility and obedience, both suburban weekend and rural ranching stockdog trialers, search and rescue workers, therapy dogs and their people, breeders committed to maintaining the versatile dog they inherited, other breeders enamored of big-coated show dogs with untested herding talent, and much more. C.A. Sharp, with her kitchen-table produced *Double Helix Network News* and the Australian Shepherd Health & Genetics Institute that she helped found—not to mention her reflection on her own practices as a breeder and her adoption of a too-small Aussie rescue pooch after the death of the last dog of her breeding—embodies for me the practice of love of a breed in its historical complexity.

Cayenne's breeders, Gayle and Shannon Oxford in California's Central Valley, are active in both the USASA and ASCA. Committed to breeding and training working stockdogs and also showing in conformation and agility, the Oxfords taught me about "the versatile Aussie," which I see as analogous to the Pyr people's "dual purpose" or "whole dog" discourse. These idioms work to prevent the splitting up of breeds into ever more isolated gene pools, each dedicated to a specialists' limited goal, whether that be agility sports, beauty, or something else. The bedrock test of an Australian Shepherd, however, remains the ability to herd with consummate skill. If "versatility" does not start there, the working breed will not survive.

A Category of One's Own

Anyone who has done historical research knows that the undocumented often have more to say about how the world is put together than do the well pedigreed. What do contemporary companion species relations between humans and "unregistered" dogs in technoculture tell us about both inheriting—or perhaps better, inhabiting—histories and also forging new possibilities? These are the dogs who need "A Category of One's Own," in honor of Virginia Woolf. Author of the famous feminist tract, "A Room of One's Own," Woolf understood what happens when the impure stroll over the lawns of the properly registered. She also understood what happens when these marked (and marking) beings get credentials and an income.

Generic scandals get my attention, especially the ones that ooze racialized sex and sexualized race for all the species involved. What should I call the categorically unfixed dogs, even if I stay only in America? Mutts, mongrels, All-Americans, random bred dogs, Heinz 57, mixed breeds, or just plain dogs? And why should categories for dogs in America be in English? Not just "the Americas," but also the United States is a highly polyglot world. Above, concentrating on Great Pyrenees and Australian Shepherds, I had to suggest the conundrums of inheriting local and global histories in modern breeds by a couple of shaggy dog stories. Similarly, here I cannot begin to plumb the histories of all the sorts of dogs that fit into neither functional kind nor institutionalized breed. And so, I will offer only one story, but one that ramifies further into webs of worldly complexity at each retelling. I will tell about Satos.

"Sato" is slang in Puerto Rico for a street dog. I learned this fact in two places: on the Internet at www.saveasato.org and in Twig Mowatt's moving essay in the Fall 2002 issue of the glossy dog cultures magazine, *Bark*. Both of these sites landed me squarely in the naturecultures of what gets politely called "modernization." "Sato" is just about the only Spanish word I learned in either site; that cued me into the direction of the semiotic and material traffic in this zone of dogland. I also figured out that Satos are capitalized, in lexical convention and monetary investment, in the process of moving from the hard streets of the southern "developing world" to the "forever homes" of the enlightened north.

At least as important, I learned that I am interpellated into this story in mind and heart. I cannot disown it by calling attention to its racially-tinged, sexually-infused, class-saturated, and colonial tones and structures. Again and again in my manifesto, I and my people need to learn to inhabit histories, not disown them, least of all through the cheap tricks of puritanical critique. In the Sato story, there are two kinds of superficially opposed temptations to puritanical critique. The first is to indulge in the colonialist sentimentality that sees only philanthropic (philocanidic?) rescue of the abused in the traffic of dogs from Puerto Rican streets to no-kill animal shelters in the United States and from there to proper homes. The second is to indulge in historical structural analysis in a way that denies both emotional bonds and material complexity and so avoids the always messy participation in action that might improve lives across many kinds of difference.

About 10,000 Puerto Rican dogs have made the transition from street life to suburban homes since 1996 when airline worker Chantal Robles of San Juan teamed up with Karen Fehrenbach, visiting the island from Arkansas, to set up the Save-a-Sato Foundation. The facts that led them to action are searing. Millions of fertile and usually diseased and starving dogs scavenge for a meal and shelter in Puerto Rico's impoverished neighborhoods, construction sites, garbage dumps, gas stations, fast food parking lots, and drug sale zones. The dogs are rural and urban, big and little, recognizably from an institutionalized breed and plainly of no breed at all. They are mostly young—feral dogs don't tend to get very old; and there are lots of puppies, both abandoned by people and born to street bitches. Official animal shelters in Puerto Rico mainly kill the dogs and cats surrendered to them or collected in their sweeps. Sometimes these swept-up animals are owned and cared for; but they live rough, vulnerable to complaint and official action. Conditions in the municipal shelters are the stuff of an animal rights horror show.

Very many dogs of all sorts in Puerto Rico are, of course, well cared for. The poor as well as the wealthy cherish animals. But if people abandon a dog, they are far more likely to let the pooch loose than bring him or her to an under-funded and poorly-staffed "shelter" that is certain to kill its charges.

Furthermore, the class-, nation-, and culture-based animal welfare ethic of sterilizing dogs and cats is not wide-spread in Puerto Rico (or in much of Europe and many places in the US). Mandatory sterilization and reproductive control have a very checkered history in Puerto Rico, even when one restricts one's historical memory to policies for non-human species. At the very least, the notion that the only proper dog is a sterile dog—except for those in the care of responsible (in whose view?) breeders—brings us smashing into the world of biopower and its technocultural apparatus in the metropole and the colonies. Puerto Rico is both metropole and colony.

None of this removes the fact that fertile feral dogs have sex, whelp lots of puppies they can't feed, and die of awful diseases in great pain and large numbers. It's not just a narrative. To make matters worse, Puerto Rico is no more free than the United States of damaged, abusing people of all social classes who inflict dire mental and physical injuries on animals both deliberately and indifferently. Homeless animals, like homeless people, are fair game in the free trade—or maybe better, free fire—zones.

The action taken by Robles, Fehrenbach, and their supporters is, to me, as inspiring as it is disturbing. They established and run a private shelter in San Juan that functions as a half-way house for dogs on their way to mostly international adoption. (But Puerto Rico is part of the United States, or is it?) The demand in Puerto Rico for these dogs is slight; that is not a natural fact, but a biopolitical one. Anyone who has thought about human international adoption knows that. The Save-a-Sato Foundation raises money, trains volunteers to bring dogs (and some cats) to the shelter without further traumatizing them, organizes Puerto Rican veterinarians who treat and sterilize animals for free, socializes the future adoptees in manners proper to the north, prepares papers for them, and arranges with the airlines to ship about thirty dogs per week on commercial flights to a network of no-kill shelters in several states, mostly in the northeast. Post 9/11, tourists flying out of San Juan are recruited to claim crates of emigrating dogs as their personal baggage so that the anti-terrorist apparatus does not shut down the rescue pipeline.

The Foundation runs an English-language website to inform its potential adopting audience and to link support groups to people who take the dogs into, in the idiom of the website, their "forever families." The website is full of successful adoption accounts, pre-adoption horror stories, before and after photos, invitations to take action and to contribute money, information for finding a Sato to adopt, and useful links to dogland cyberculture.

A person in Puerto Rico can become a member of the Save-a-Sato Foundation by rescuing a minimum of five dogs per month. Volunteers mainly pay whatever it costs out of their own pockets. They find, feed, and gentle dogs before urging them into crates and taking them to the half-way house. Puppies and youngsters are the first priority, but not the only ones picked up. Dogs who are too sick to get well are euthanized, but many severely injured and ill dogs recover and get placed. All sorts of people become volunteers. The website tells about one elderly woman on social security living close to homelessness herself who recruited homeless people to gentle and collect dogs, for whom she paid $5 each out of her meager funds. Knowing the genre of such a story does not mute its power—or its truth. The photos on the site seem to be mostly of middle-class Puerto Rican women, but heterogeneity in the Save-a-Sato Foundation is not reserved for the dogs.

The airplane is an instrument in a series of subject-transforming technologies. The dogs who come out of the belly of the plane are subject to a different social contract than the one they were born into. However, not just any Puerto Rican stray is likely to get its second birth from this aluminum womb. Smallish dogs, like girls in the human scene, are the gold standard in the dog adoption market. US fear of aggression from the Other knows few bounds, and certainly not those of species or sex. To follow this point, we need to get from the airport to the excellent shelter in Sterling, Massachusetts, which has placed more than 2000 Satos (and about 100 cats) since it joined the program in 1999. Once again, I find my bearings in dogland's exuberant cyberculture (www.sterlingshelter.org).

Animal shelters in the US northeast in general have too few dogs in the 10-35 pound range to fill the demand. Being the owner (or guardian) of a mid-sized, sterilized, rescue-derived, well-behaved dog confers high status in much of US dogland. Some of this status comes from pride in not succumbing to the eugenic discourses that continue to luxuriate in purebred dog worlds. But adoption of a street or thrown-away dog, mutt or not, hardly removes one from the swamps of class- and culture-rooted "improving" ideologies, familial biopolitics, and pedagogical fashions. Indeed, eugenics and the other improving discourses of "modern" life have so many shared ancestors (and living siblings) that the coefficient of inbreeding exceeds that of even father-daughter couplings.

Adopting a shelter dog takes a lot of work, a fair amount of money (but not as much as it costs to prepare the dogs), and a willingness to submit to a governing apparatus sufficient to activate the allergies of any Foucauldian or garden-variety libertarian. I support that apparatus—and many other kinds of institutionalized power—to protect classes of subjects, including dogs. I also vigorously support adopting rescue and shelter animals. And so my dyspepsia at recognizing where all this comes from will have to be endured rather than relieved.

Good shelters get lots of requests for Sato dogs. Getting such a dog keeps people from buying from pet stores and supporting the puppy mill industry. The Sterling shelter tells us that 99% of puppies brought to it from the US are medium to large dogs, all of whom get adopted. Many largish puppies and youngsters come into the Sterling haven from the Homebound Hounds Program, which imports thrown-away dogs to the northeast from cooperating shelters in the US south—another area of the world where the ethic of sterilizing dogs and cats is not secure, to say the least. Still, people looking for smaller shelter dogs are largely out of luck in the domestic market. These folks' family enlargement strategies require different layers of locals and globals. However, just as with international adoption of children, it is not easy to get an imported dog. Detailed interviews and forms, home visits, references from friends and veterinarians, promises to educate the dog properly, counseling from on-site trainers, proof of home ownership or written documentation from landlords that pets are allowed, and then long waiting lists: all this, and more, is normal. The goal is a permanent home for the dogs.

The means is a kinship-making apparatus that reaches into and draws from the history of "the family" in every imaginable way, literally. Proof of the effectiveness of the companion-species, family-making apparatus is to be found in a little narrative analysis. Adoption success stories regularly refer to siblings and other multi-species kin as mom, dad, sister, brother, aunt, uncle, cousin, godfather, etc. Purebred adoption stories do the same thing, and these adoption/ownership processes involve many of the same documentary and social instruments before one can qualify to get a dog. It is nearly impossible—and generally irrelevant—to read from the stories what species is being referred to. A pet bird is the sister of a new dog, and the human baby brother and aged cat aunt all are represented to relate to the human adults of the house as moms and/or dads. Heterosexuality is not germane; heterospecificity is.

I resist being called the "mom" to my dogs because I fear infantilization of the adult canines and misidentification of the important fact that I wanted dogs, not babies. My multi-species family is not about surrogacy and substitutes; we are trying to live other tropes, other metaplasms. We need other nouns and pronouns for the kin genres of companion species, just as we did (and still do) for the spectrum of genders. Except in a party invitation or a philosophical discussion, "significant other" won't do for human sexual partners; and the term performs little better to house the daily meanings of cobbled together kin relations in dogland.

But perhaps I worry about words too much. I have to admit that it is not clear that the conventional kin idioms in use in US dogland refer to age, species, or biological reproductive status much at all (except to require that most of the non-humans be sterile). Genes are not the point, and that surely is a relief. The point is companion-species making. It's all in the family, for better and for worse, until death do us part. This is a family made up in the belly of the monster of inherited histories that have to be inhabited to be transformed. I always knew that if I turned up pregnant, I wanted the being in my womb to be a member of another species; maybe that turns out to be the general condition. It's not just mutts, in or out of the traffic of international adoption, who seek a category of one's own in significant otherness.

I yearn for much more reflection in dogland about what it means to inherit the multi-species, relentlessly complex legacy that crosses evolutionary, personal, and historical time scales of companion species. Every registered breed, indeed every dog, is immersed in practices and stories that can and should tie dog people into myriad histories of living labor, class formations, gender and sexual elaborations, racial categories, and other layers of locals and globals. Most dogs on earth are not members of institutionalized breeds. Village dogs and rural and urban feral dogs carry their own signifying otherness for the people they live among, and not just for people like me. Nor are mutts or so-called "random bred" dogs in the "developed world" like the functional kinds of dogs that emerged in economies and ecologies that no longer flourish. Puerto Rican strays called "Satos" become members of Massachusetts "forever families" out of histories of stunning complexity and consequence. In current naturecultures, breeds might be a necessary, if deeply flawed, means to continue the useful kinds of dogs they came from. Current US ranchers have more to fear from real estate developers from San Francisco or Denver than from wolves, no matter how far they get from the parks, or from Native Americans, no matter how effective they are in court.

In my own personal-historical natureculture, I know in my flesh that the largely middle-class, white people of Pyr and Aussie land have an as yet unarticulated responsibility to participate in re-imagining grasslands ecologies and ways of life that were blasted in significant part by the very ranching practices that required the work of these dogs. Through their dogs, people like me are tied to indigenous sovereignty rights, ranching economic and ecological survival, radical reform of the meat-industrial complex, racial justice, the consequences of war and migration, and the institutions of technoculture. It's about, in Helen Verran's words, "getting on together." When "pure-bred" Cayenne, "mixed-breed" Roland, and I touch, we embody in the flesh the connections of the dogs and the people who made us possible. When I stroke my landmate Susan Caudill's sensuous Great Pyrenees, Willem, I also touch relocated Canadian gray wolves, upscale Slovakian bears, and international restoration ecology, as well as dog shows and multi-national pastoral economies. Along with the whole dog, we need the whole legacy, which is, after all, what makes the whole companion species possible. Not so oddly, all those wholes are non-Euclidean knots of partial connections. Inhabiting that legacy without the pose of innocence, we might hope for the creative grace of play.

From "Notes of a Sports Writer's Daughter," *June 2000:*

> *Ms Cayenne Pepper has shown her true species being at last. She's a female Klingon in heat. You may not watch much television or be a fan of the Star Trek universe like I am, but I'll bet the news that Klingon females are formidable sexual beings, whose tastes run to the ferocious, has reached everyone in the federated planets. The Pyr on our land, the intact 20-month-old Willem, has been Cayenne's playmate since they were both puppies, beginning at about 4 months of age. Cayenne was spayed when she was 6 1/2 months old. She's always happily humped her way down Willem's soft and inviting backside, starting at his head with her*

nose pointed to his tail, while he lies on the ground
trying to chew her leg or lick a rapidly passing genital
area. But during our Memorial weekend stay on the
Healdsburg land, things heated up, put mildly. Willem
is a randy, gentle, utterly inexperienced, adolescent male
soul. Cayenne does not have an estrus hormone in her
body (but let us not forget those very much present
adrenal cortices pumping out so-called androgens that
get lots of the credit for juicing up mammalian desire in
males and females). She is, however, one turned on little
bitch with Willem, and he is INTERESTED. She does
not do this with any other dog, 'intact' or not. None of
their sexual play has anything to do with remotely functional heterosexual mating behavior—no efforts of
Willem to mount, no presenting of an attractive female
backside, not much genital sniffing, no whining and
pacing, none of all that reproductive stuff. No, here we
have pure polymorphous perversity that is so dear to the
hearts of all of us who came of age in the 1960s reading
Norman O. Brown.

The 110-pound Willem lies down with a bright
look in his eye. Cayenne, weighing in at 35 pounds,
looks positively crazed as she straddles her genital area
on top of his head, her nose pointed toward his tail,
presses down and wags her backside vigorously. I mean
hard and fast. He tries for all he's worth to get his
tongue on her genitals, which inevitably dislodges her
from the top of his head. It looks a bit like the rodeo,
with her riding a bronco and staying on as long as
possible. They have slightly different goals in this game,
but both are committed to the activity. Sure looks like
eros to me. Definitely not agape. They keep this up for
about three minutes to the exclusion of any other
activity. Then they go back to it for another round. And
another. Susan's and my laughing, whether raucous or
discrete, does not merit their attention. Cayenne growls

like a female Klingon during the activity, teeth bared. Remember how many times the half-Klingon B'Elanna Torres on Star Trek Voyager *put her human flyboy lover Tom Paris in sickbay? Cayenne's playing, but oh my, what a game. Willem is earnestly intent. He is not a Klingon, but what feminists of my generation would call a considerate lover.*

Their youth and vitality make a mockery of reproductive heterosexual hegemony, as well as of abstinence-promoting gonadectomies. Now, I, of all people, who have written infamous books about how we Western humans project our social orders and desires onto animals without scruple, should know better than to see confirmation of Norman O. Brown's Love's Body *in my spayed Aussie dynamo and Susan's talented Landscape Guardian Dog with that big, sloppy, velvety tongue. Still, what else could be going on? Hint: this is not a game of fetch or chase.*

No, this is ontological choreography, which is that vital sort of play that the participants invent out of the histories of body and mind they inherit and that they rework into the fleshly verbs that make them who they are. They invented this game; this game remodels them. Metaplasm, once again. It always comes back to the biological flavor of the important words. The word is made flesh in mortal naturecultures. ■

Look for these titles by Prickly Paradigm, and others to come: